HIGHER BUREAUCRACY AND DEVELOPMENT

Higher Bureaucracy and Development

Rs. 690

ISBN:81-7835-523-X

Published in 2007 in India by
Kalpaz Publications
C-30, Satyawati Nagar,
Delhi-110052
E-mail: kalpaz@hotmail.com

Lasser Type Setting by: Rudra Computer Graphics, Delhi
Printed at : Salasar Imaging System, Delhi

Contents

Abbreviations

ABVP	: Akhila Bharatiya Vidhyarthi Parishad
ARC	: Administrative Reforms Commission
BDO	: Block Development Officer
BJP	: Bharatiya Janatha Party
CADA	: Command Area Development Agency
CAG	: Comptroller and Auditor General
CDP	: Community Development Programme
CPI	: Communist Party of India
CPI (M)	: Communist Party of India (Marxist)
DDP	: Desert Development Programme
DPAP	: Drought Prone Area Programme
DRDA	: District Rural Development Agency
DWCRA	: Development of Women and Children in Rural Areas
GATT	: General Agreement on Tariff and Trade
IAS	: Indian Administrative Service
ICDS	: Integrated Child Development Service

ICS : Indian Civil Service

IFS : Indian Forest Service

IIT : Indian Institute of Technology

IMF : International Monitory Fund

INC : Indian National Congress

IPS : Indian Police Service

IRDP : Integrated Rural Development Programme

JRY : Jawahar Rosgar Yojana

KPCC : Kerala Pradesh Congress Committee

KSEB : Kerala State Electricity Board

KSIDC : Kerala State Industrial Development Corporation

KSU : Kerala Students Union

KSRTC : Kerala State Road Transport Corporation

LDF : Left Democratic Front

M : Malayalam

MFAL : Marginal Farmers and Agricultural Labour Development

NDP : National Democratic Party

NES : National Extension Service

NGO : Non Gazetted Officer/ Non Governmental Organization

NREP : National Rural Employment Programme

NRI : Non Resident Indian

NSS : Nair Service Society

NSU : National Students Union

PDS : Public Distribution System

PSC : Public Service Commission

PWD : Public Works Department

REC : Regional Engineering College

RLEGP : Rural Landless Employment Generation Programme

RTO : Regional Transport Office

SC : Scheduled Caste

SFDA : Small Farmers Development Agency

SFI : Students Federation of India

SNDP : Sree Narayana Dharma Paripalana Yogam

SRP : Socialist Revolutionary Party

SSLC : Secondary School Leaving Certificate

ST	: Scheduled Tribe
TRYSEM	: Training of Rural Youth in Self Employment
UDF	: United Democratic Front
UPSC	: Union Public Service Commission
VMFT	: Vakkom Moulavi Foundation Trust

List of Figures

List of Tables

Foreword

Bureaucracy as a part of state apparatus has been playing a critical role in the socio-economic transformation and development of all societies. Although, politicians are in command, it is the higher civil servants who provide input into various development policies and schemes. Their deep understanding and experience would benefit the political leadership in the correct formulation of development strategies. While the bureaucracy shows an elitist attitude, it has over the years learnt to play a positive role in society. Kerala is one of the few states in India where political parties with different and distinct political ideologies like CPM and congress led Governments have formulated policies for bringing about socio-economic changes on the basis of their own ideologies.

In the above context, Dr. Jitha has made an attempt to examine, the socio-economic and educational background of the higher bureaucracy in Kerala, how far the higher bureaucrats became development oriented, critically evaluate their role in the formulation and implementation of development policies in the state, discussed the relationship between political leadership and the higher bureaucracy by identifying and studying certain areas of conflict, study citizens grievances with administration, assess their attitude towards people by examining the micro level study of a major developmental policy namely IRDP, examine whether there is nexus between bureaucrats and dominant socio-economic groups in the rural areas with a view to find out who appropriate the fruits of development plans, critically examine whether higher bureaucracy has been functional or dys-functional to the new liberal economic and administrative policies and find out the need for evolving and developing a new bureaucratic culture, which is people oriented and development oriented.

The study establishes the fact that higher bureaucracy has been playing a very dominant role in the formulation and implementation of development projects. This is because the political leadership mostly depends on the bureaucracy for giving shape to their programme and policies. However, the bureaucracy is yet to become development and people oriented. In this context it is important to note that International Agencies, Planning Commission, Finance Commission etc. determine major policies and the officers are supposed to implement them at the state level. The study also reveals that there is political interference and it is affecting the implementation of developmental programmes. The officers who are hard working, enterprising and having enough vision are not allowed to continue in the same office, if they resist such political interference. At the same time politico-bureaucratic strata exercise power and try to maximize individual advantage for personal benefit. The author establishes these facts with enough factual data.

Regarding the role of bureaucracy in development administration, they co-ordinate and supervise various administrative programme of the government. But the bureaucracy is out of touch with the real needs of the people and people lack confidence in these officers. It is unfortunate to note that the development programmes aimed to eradicate rural poverty like IRDP has not benefited the people because of lack of co-ordination, lack of proper planning, political interference and other vested interests. This has been agreed by the people, politicians as well as bureaucrats in the survey. The common man have the feeling that bureaucracy is more inclined towards the rich and influential sections of the society. The author in her study concludes that, the elitist character of the bureaucracy is still persists with all its manifestations.

All the chapters are well presented in a simple and lucid language. The findings and interpretation are well supported by primary and secondary source of data for which the author deserves appreciation. It is also noteworthy that this research work has thrown light into some unexplored areas of public administration which will be helpful to further research in this field. This book is based on the doctoral thesis on the same subject submitted to Kerala University by the author. I am sure that, this book will be quite useful to anyone dealing with public administration. I congratulate the author for bringing out such a nice piece of work.

Thiruvananthapuram
July 21, 2006

Prof. (Dr.) N. Babu
Former Vice-Chancellor, University of Kerala
and
Former
Vice- Chairman
Kerala State Higher Education Council

Preface

The role of state administration and issues of development are core issues that are being seriously discussed and debated with a view to redefine their role in the context of the fast changing socio-economic and political situations. This quest for re-definition of these concepts is largely a corollary of the liberalization, privatization and globalization policies persuaded by the government since 1991. These new socio-economic policies coupled with immense possibilities opened up by information technology have indeed necessitated the need for developing a new administrative outlook and strategy. So that the administration could be geared to suit the developmental needs of society. This shift in the developmental paradigm of the bureaucracy has to be realised without undermining the question of equality and social justice. It is therefore significant to study how the bureaucracy that has been characterized as elitistic and not development and people oriented would function in the context of liberalization as a potent instrument for development.

The new socio-economic and administrative reform initiated by the central government has percolated down to the state level. It is important to note that most of the state governments have also introduced this liberalization agenda not only in the economic field but also in the administrative field. Accordingly, Kerala state has also introduced reform at the economic and administrative levels. It is in this context of the developmental agenda that the role of higher bureaucracy as the principal instrument for implementing these new economic and administrative policies, the higher bureaucracy has been chosen as the subject of this study. In particular, the study has examined from a developmental perspective, the role of higher bureaucracy in the socio-economic development of the state. The importance of the study lies in the fact that higher bureaucracy, in spite of a highly developed political culture and consciousness, has been playing a predominant role in the formulation and implementation of developmental policies. No serious research has been done on the subject. Hence this study is important.

The main objectives of this study are:

(1) To find out the socio-economic and educational background of the higher bureaucracy in Kerala.

(2) To examine how far the higher bureaucrats become development oriented, shedding their colonial legacy.

(3) To critically evaluate its role in the formulation and implementation of developmental policies in the state.

(4) To discuss the relationship between political leadership and the higher bureaucracy by identifying and studying certain important areas of conflict.

(5) To study the citizen's grievances with administration.

(6) To assess their attitude towards the people by examining the micro level study of a major developmental policy namely Integrated Rural Development Programme.

(7) To examine whether there is nexus between bureaucrats and dominant socio-economic groups in the rural and urban areas with a view to find out who appropriates the fruits of developmental plans.

(8) To critically examine whether higher bureaucracy has been functional or dysfunctional to the new liberal economic and administrative policies.

(9) To find out the need for evolving and developing a new bureaucratic culture, which is both people oriented and development oriented.

With a view to study the core question and issues involved in the subject, few important hypotheses have been formulated for empirical substantiation. They include :

(1) The higher bureaucracy in Kerala continues to remain elitist in character in terms of their socio-economic backgrounds, attitudes and values.

(2) The impartiality and commitment of the bureaucracy towards people's issue have been largely compromised by the bureaucracy.

(3) The political neutrality, which used to be the characteristic feature of the bureaucracy has been lost its relevance and importance in the context of the coalition politics of the state.

(4) Their attitudes towards people have not undergone any significant change.

(5) Higher bureaucracy in Kerala has largely committed to the new liberal and economic policies that have been implemented in the state.

Review of Literature

Regarding the academic significance of this study, it may be stated that, there is hardly any work covering the higher bureaucracy in Kerala and its role in developmental process. There are several works that deals with bureaucracy and development. The studies done earlier on higher bureaucracy have a national level focus. At the same time there are some scholarly works having direct bearing on the subject. The Administrators in a Changing Society (C.P.Bhambhri, 1972), Bureaucrats Under Stress (Richard.P.Taub, 1969), The Role of Higher Civil Service in India (Dwarakadas, 1958), Administrative Development in India (Premalatha Bansal, 1974), Administrators in a Developing Society (Retna Bhattacharya, 1989), Bureaucracy and Administration- Studies in Policy Performance and Reform (B.R. Verma, 1998), Indian Bureaucracy Through the Ages (Satish Tiwari, 1999), Bureaucracy and Administrative System (Sharda Goswami, 1998), Bureaucracy and Developmént Administration (Pai Panandikar and S.S Kshir Sagar,1978), Public Administration in India-21st Century Challenges for Good Governance (R.B. Jain, 2002), Challenges and Changes in Administrative System (I.C.Srivastava,1999), and Development Administration (R.K. Sapru,1994) are some of the scholarly works directly related to higher bureaucracy and development in India. These scholarly works provided some of the basic material for the present study. In addition, some of the scholarly works of foreign authors on bureaucracy like Bureaucracy and Political Development (Joseph La Palombara,1965), The Theory of Social and Economic Organization (Max Weber,1947), Bureaucracy and Modern Society (Peter Blaue,1965), Bureaucratic Phenomena

(Michel Crozzier,1964), Development Administration in Asia (Edward Weidner,1970), Approaches to Development-Politics Administration and Change (John Montgomery, 1966) also helped for getting a theoretical base for this study.

Regarding the higher bureaucracy in Kerala there is no serious study. However, there are few works on the subject. No doctoral thesis has been done earlier on this important subject. A perusal of the available literature on bureaucracy in Kerala clearly reveals that these were mostly historical and general in character and not problem oriented empirical micro level study.

S.N. Sadasivan's two works (1) Administration and Social Development in Kerala (1986), and (2) Administrative Integration of Kerala (1986) are important studies. Administration and Social Development in Kerala explores the sociological base of administration and the major communities, which control and influence the administrative behaviour. The author examines the inter-relationship of administration and society and in particular how the dominant community could wheel tremendous powers and influence on administration. The author argues that any failure of the administration to adopt itself to the changing needs of the society would result in increased social conflict and tension. In the book Administrative Integration of Kerala, the author briefly discusses the problem of integration of the administrative services in the erstwhile princely sates of Travancore-Cochin and Malabar. K. Sukumaran Nair in his book, Administrative Coordination at State Level- A Study of Government Secretariat and Board of Revenue in Kerala offers a historical overview of Secretariat and Board of Revenue in order to illuminate the nature of administrative coordination at the state level. The Administrative Reforms Commission Report while historically evaluating the administrative structure and performance put forward a number of suggestions for the improvement and performance of administration which inter-alia includes the need for the creation of Kerala Civil Service. Kerala State Gazetteer, a Government publication contained some aspects of the history and development of administration. So it is thus evident that no serious research has been done on higher bureaucracy in Kerala especially on its development role.

The methodology of this study is both historical and analytical. A historical dimension has built into the study in order to illuminate the nature and character of the present bureaucracy in the contemporary Kerala. However, the study is mainly analytical in the sense that the logical and casual connections have been established between facts. Both primary and secondary sources have been explored for the completion of the study. The primary sources include official records, commission reports, *Kerala Legislative Assembly Debates, Planning Board Evaluation Reports, Autobiographies etc.* Data have also been collected through field study and interviews with higher bureaucrats, politicians and people on the basis of three different sets of structured questionnaire. The names of the Civil Servents were collected from the IAS Gradation list of 1994 and 2001. About ninety higher civil servants from Kerala cadre and about fifty political leaders including ministers, former ministers, legislatures and local body members have been interviewed. The names of the civil servants were not included in the text as per their requests. The data about the developmental role of bureaucracy and its attitude towards people have been collected from a micro level study of the IRDP beneficiaries in Thiruvananthapuram District. Two hundred beneficiaries of IRDP have been identified by applying simple random sampling technique and interviewed to find out its impact. Books, articles in research journals, unpublished doctoral thesis, newspaper, website etc. constitutes secondary sources of data.

This book has been structured into seven chapters. The first chapter discusses various concepts and theories relating to the role of higher bureaucracy in the development of Kerala. They include the Concept of Bureaucracy, Development Bureaucracy, Development Administration, Socio Economic Change, Nexus Between Politics and Administration and Bureaucracy and Common Man. The focus of the second chapter is on the socio-political and administrative context in which the higher bureaucracy functions. The socio economic and educational background of higher bureaucracy has been discussed in the third chapter with a view to understand the social base of bureaucracy and their changing attitude and perception. In the fourth chapter an attempt is made to evaluate the role of higher bureaucracy in the formulation and implementation of policies. The focus of the fifth chapter is on the relationship between the politicians and higher bureaucrats in the specific context of Kerala's coalition politics. The sixth chapter analyses the bureaucracy's attitudes and perception towards the people and the people's attitude towards bureaucracy, in a highly literate and politically conscious state. In the final chapter the major findings and suggestions for future research have been discussed.

Acknowledgements

This book is largely based on my doctoral dissertation submitted to the University of Kerala. In preparing this work I have received guidance and assistance from several people and institutions. I sincerely express my deep sense of gratitude and respect to my teacher and research guide **Professor (Dr.) M. Bhaskaran Nair**, former Professor and Head, Department of Political Science, University of Kerala for his valuable guidance and constant encouragement throughout my Ph. D. programme and preparation of this book. I am deeply indebted to him for initiating me into this subject. His immense insight, creative criticism and appreciation, courtesy and humane feelings made the completion of this task relatively easy.

I wish to express my heartfelt gratitude to my teacher, Prof. (Dr.) N.K Bhaskaran, former Head, Department of Political Science, University of Kerala for the encouragement in this work. I am thankful to my teachers Prof. (Dr.) G.

Gopakumar, Professor and Head, Dr. J. Prabhash and other faculty members, Department of Political Science, University of Kerala, for the support. The timely help and suggestions received from Dr. Shaji Varkey, Sr. Lecturer, Department of Political Science is gratefully acknowledged.

I express my deep sense of gratitude to all IAS officers who cooperated with this study, particularly Shri. Vinod Ray, Dr. D. Babu Paul, Shri. T.N. Jayachadran, Shri. C.P. Nair, Shri. M.P. Joseph, Late Dr. V. Rajagopal, Shri. K. Jayakumar, Shri. E.K. Bharat Bhooshan, Shri. Sajan Peter, Shri. G. Gopalakrishna Pillai, Shri. John Mathai, Shri.K.J. Mathew, Shri. K.J. Alphons, Shri. P.J. Thomas, Shri P.K. Mohanthi, Shri. Viswas Mehtha, Shri. Dinesh Sharma, Shri. Rajeev Sadanandan, Shri.U.K.S. Chouhan, Shri. L. Nadarajan, Dr. V. Venu, Smt. J. Lalithambika, Smt. K.B. Valsala Kumari, Smt. Lida Jacob, Smt. Aruna Sundararajan, Smt. Sarada Muraleedharan etc. who in spite of their busy schedule willingly filled in the questionnaire with their detailed comments. The encouragement they made at the time of data collection is gratefully acknowledged.

The valuable suggestions and help received from former Minister for Agriculture, Smt. K.R. Gouriamma and former Chief Minister Shri. Oommen Chandy MLA are gratefully acknowledged. I am also thankful to all the politicians who filled in the questionnaire in particular former Minister K.C. Venugopal MLA,

K.P. Kunjikkannan, ex-MLA and C. Jyothi, former Chairperson, Payyannur Municipality who shared their deep insights.

I am also thankful to the Kazhakkoottam and Vellanad Block staff. The help and assistance rendered in the field study by Smt. Santhakumary, VEO, Kazhakkoottam Block is worth remembering. Here I express my sense of gratitude to the beneficiaries of IRDP of Kazhakkoottam and Vellanad Blocks with whose cooperation I completed this work.

The help in material collection rendered by Library and office staff Dept. of Political Science is gratefully acknowledged. I am also thankful to the staff of Campus Library, University Library, Centre for Development Studies, Ulloor, Legislative Library and Institute of Management in Government for the help rendered.

Here I record my gratitude to Prof. (Dr.) N. Babu, former Vice chancellor, University of Kerala for the critical evaluation of this book and writing the foreword.

I am grateful to the University Grants Commission for the award of a Teacher Fellowship. My thanks are also due to Manager, Sree Narayana Trusts, Kollam for kindly relieving me from duty for the completion of this work.

I express my deep sense of regard to my mother Smt. G. Sujatha for the support in this endeavour. My husband Dr. A. Thulaseedharan was a constant source of encouragement and inspiration to make this endeavour a reality. My deep sense of gratitude is expressing here. I also thank my in-laws for their encouragement and loving care. Finally, I thank all those who helped me in different ways in completing this work.

Above all, I bow before the Almighty God who made this endeavour a success.

(Jitha S.R)

1

Bureaucracy and Development-A Theoretical Frame Work

The higher bureaucracy, which is an integral part of an organized government, plays a crucial role in the socio-economic development of a country. When the government is involved in developmental activities, bureaucracy becomes the main instrument of the implementation of government programmes. The higher bureaucracy is defined as a relatively permanent top group of civil servants who are placed between the political decision makers and the rank-and file bureaucracy and who share in different degrees the task of directing various administrative agencies[1].

India is a democratic, secular state with a representative system of governance. The state is confronted with multi-dimensional challenges like growing incidence of social and political violence, communalism, regionalism, linguism and regional disparities on account of neo-liberal economic policies. Besides, the Indian state has to safeguard the sovereignty of the country against foreign intervention and economic exploitation. The constitutional framework and the legal structure fail when strong interest groups in politics, society and economy establish their firm control. India's relative power in the international sphere has declined. It could neither translate its human capital nor natural resources into productive assets to claim a legitimate place in the world.

In a developing country like India, bureaucracy is considered as the backbone of developmental programmes. The civil servants who are engaged in development activities constitute the development bureaucracy. The responsibility of bringing about socio-economic change has fallen upon the higher bureaucracy, which is permanent in nature. The success of developmental programmes depends upon the ability of the civil servants to understand the problems of development and modernization. In this context bureaucracy can be eminently functional or abysmally dysfunctional.

Indian bureaucracy is the result of two different sets of influences, the British tradition and democratic welfarist tradition of the post-independence period. India, which had inherited the British administrative system of the colonial time, had a bureaucracy that conforms to the classical pattern described by Max Weber, the German sociologist[2]. The British who ruled India for almost a couple of centuries established a system of bureaucracy, the key features were elitism and an unchanging hierarchical structure. The British bureaucracy in India was designed to serve limited purposes and closed its eyes on nation building. Such a system was unsuitable for independent India.

In India, the bureaucratic system dates back to the Northcote Trevelyan Report of 1854[3]. It resulted in the recruitment of a set of administrators for India from Oxford and Cambridge Universities designated as the Indian Civil Service, the ICS. The Indian Administrative Service constituted after independence is a successor to the Indian Civil Service. Certain changes have made in the training programme and orientation of the new services, but the major traits and structural patterns remained the same.

A sustained programme of economic development is the main objective of any country. Development has affected every sphere of human activity like industry, technology, education, agriculture and administration[4]. For achieving economic progress the complex task of planning has to be undertaken. These followed a centralized system of planning (Five Year Plans), launching of multipurpose irrigation and power projects, giant industrial complexes in the public sector etc. These expanding frontiers of development required an administrative state able to handle social, economic, political and scientific problems efficiently and expeditiously. Bureaucracy has thus become one of the chief instruments in the hands of government to deal with the challenges of a new political order and socio-economic advancement[5]. The higher bureaucrats participate not only in the policy making but also act as the link between the ministers and the implementing agencies. They play a decisive role in nation-building and its performance depends upon the success or failure of various programmes of socio-economic development. Therefore, the role of higher bureaucracy is especially important in India. However, since the end of colonial period it has been popularly and persistently argued that Indian administration retain some of the negative aspect of imperial legacy such as elitism, status consciousness, aloofness, lack of dedication and authoritarianism. During the British days they were both policy makers and the executers[6]. However, the British bureaucracy was not subjected to popular scrutiny, hence failed to feel the pulse of the people.

The hopes and aspirations of the people of independent India created new tasks and responsibilities, which were assigned to the newly created IAS, successor of ICS, but with no radical break with the British administrative tradition. Sardar Vallabh Bhai Patel, the Deputy Prime Minister and Minister of Home, had emphasized the necessity of qualified administrators to maintain continuity in administration, stability and order to build a new India had rendered the process of transition smooth by his apprehension of patriotism, loyalty and the ability of new elite cadre[7]. In the post independent India, IAS has emerged as the elite corps to man the important decision making positions in the administrative system. The pattern of IAS supremacy is also visible in the state government and local bodies. Today the IAS is the core of the country's administrative structure, sharing its tasks with a number of all-India central and state services and providing strong administrative links throughout the country[8].

According to P.C. Alexander "with independence and adoption of planned economic development the content and task of Indian bureaucracy have undergone changes. Even though the civil service which independent India inherited had been designed to serve the interests of the colonial power, the leaders of the new nation were convinced that with a suitable orientation and redefinition of the role of civil service, the old administrative system could be effectively be used to serve the requirements of the sovereign democratic republic which was being established. Thus the new role of civil service was that it should serve the basic objectives laid down in the Preamble of the Constitution namely to secure for all its citizens: justice, social, economic and political, liberty of thoughts, expression, beliefs, faiths and worship, equality of status and opportunity and to promote among them all, fraternity assuring their dignity of the individual and the unity and integrity of the nation. Article

38 of the Constitution had proclaimed as a directive principle of state policy, that the state shall strives to promote the welfare of the people by securing and protecting as effectively as it may a social order in which justice, social, economic and political shall inform all the institutions of national life"[9].

With this aim, India launched a massive programme of Community Development to liberate millions of people from poverty, illiteracy ignorance, unemployment, diseases, over population etc. With the adoption of National Planning, the government sought to ensure social equality and economic justice to every citizen of the country. This change had brought about new responsibilities pertaining to economic development and social welfare on the shoulders of higher bureaucrats[10]. People who worked very closely with higher civil servants testify the lack of orientation and vision on the part of higher civil servants over the past 52 years. They continue to exist more or less in the same shape as it existed during the British period. It should be noted that most of the administrative procedures are negative in character and aimed at checking the lower level administration. They did not reach the grass roots to touch the life of the common-man. It did not come to grip with the political, economic and social problems of the masses. It was formed as a self contained system restoring all innovations and changes. When the bureaucracy is being directed by out dated rules and time consuming procedures, it hinders the development and renders administration ineffective.

The new policies of economic reform and liberalization downgrade the role of state and its instruments, chiefly the bureaucracy. In a country like India where the poor and downtrodden would require massive state support, any attempt at downsizing the bureaucracy or substituting it with private or NGO sector would be counterproductive in the long run. This has been established in several studies[11]. Very little thoughts have been given to capacity building of government functionaries with a view to improving their performance. Corruption today is on the increase in political and bureaucratic level. Corruption at all levels has become a low risk and high reward activity. It is at the state level where development administration is mainly taken place. So it is essential that the studies to explore the attitude of higher bureaucracy relating to major issues of development should be undertaken in each of the Indian states.

One of the smallest states in India, Kerala has always been in the news for more than one reason. It voted overwhelmingly against the one party dominant system of congress party and in favour of a communist government. The state has witnessed the largest number of governments, high level of institutionalization of various socio-economic interests and high literacy rate. Chronic ministerial instability especially the first four decades after independence led to the pre-occupation of political parties with parliamentary maneuvers, factionalism and spread of communalism. This enabled the higher bureaucracy to play a greater and significant role in policy formulation. The elite groups in new forms had emerged as the heads of Development Administration, various Administrative Reform Committee, District Development Committee, Panchayati Raj Institutions and other Commissions for Backward Classes[12]. The socio-cultural and economic milieu of the society, political and ministerial instability, the coalition system of government etc. lead to the bureaucratization of administration in the state, which was eventually got politicised.

Since the formation of Kerala as a separate state there has been a good deal of concern about the need to develop its economy and to improve its infra-structural facilities to resolve poverty, unemployment, power crisis, water supply, poor sanitation, transportation, lack of industrialization and faulty supply of raw materials[13]. The state has not been able to arrest the rising prices of essential commodities, resolve the problems of unemployment, and diminishing prices of agricultural products. The administration has also to be faced with new challenges like neo-liberal policy of disinvestments, attempt to restructure and downsize the bureaucracy and a series of strikes by the government servants.

Development is the top priority of every government. Development administration is the task of organizing public agencies to facilitate and implement development programmes. The major internal causes of underdevelopment are traditionalism, widespread poverty, unemployment, inefficiency and the corrupt politico- bureaucratic leadership. This politico- bureaucratic structure of society plays an important role in managing public affairs by regulating the production system and by intervening in the conflictual social process. They exercise power to manage society and also to maximize individual advantage for personal benefits. At the same time the success of the programme or project is related to implementation of developmental measures in a democratic way. Political leaders demand commitment by administrators to implement development programmes. On several occasions ministers including chief minister have publicly expressed dissatisfaction with the higher bureaucracy's behaviour. They characterize the negative character of bureaucracy in the socio-economic development of the state government. This elitist and conservative out look of the bureaucracy has retarded the progress of the state. At the same time the bureaucrats complain that there are unnecessary political and ministerial interference in the implementation of development programmes. Thus the decision makers and administrators have yet to come to grips with the real nature of development in Kerala.

Again a feeling has grown among the public that the higher bureaucrats are in league with their political masters, industrial and business classes and vested interests and is together looting the country. They forget the people who are supposed to be the supreme sovereign in a parliamentary democracy. At no time in the past so many senior bureaucrats and ministers face criminal procedures and anti-corruption enquiries.

The role of bureaucracy in a modern democracy cannot be studied in isolation and has got to be studied in all its interconnections with surrounding areas. This means that higher bureaucracy functions in a larger socio-political context and its behaviour are largely a product of multiplicity of determinants – economic, political, ideological, caste and ethnic factors. Therefore, any understanding of higher bureaucracy and its role in development in a specific socio-historic context requires a scientific and holistic approach.

In order to understand bureaucracy and its role in development process, it is imperative to define the concepts used in this book. An attempt is therefore made to examine these concepts for illuminating the study on higher bureaucracy in Kerala.

Bureaucracy

Bureaucracy has been used in so many ways. In the simple sense it denotes a body of regular government employees mostly in the specific sense of the civil service, especially the higher government service[14]. The person first used this word by speaking of it as bureaucratic was Vincent de Gournay, an eighteenth century French minister of commerce. The new word gained acceptance and soon spread to other countries. It came into considerable vogue in the nineteenth century Germany where a highly developed civil service existed. The real flowering of the word in many languages and the systematic description and analyses of bureaucracy as a part of modern government is a recent development[15].

Bureaucracy has also been used to refer to rational organization, organizational efficiency, rule by officials, public administration, modern society, top civil service etc. Thus the meaning of bureaucracy depends upon the intention of the user. The classical writings on bureaucracy can be traced to several sources. The major contribution has come from Max Weber, Karl Marx, R. Michel, Peter Blaue and others.

The concept of bureaucracy has been fully developed by Max Weber. He may be regarded as the founder of the systematic study on bureaucracy. Weber defined bureaucracy as a legal, rational, organization based on certain important characteristics like division of labour, fixed remuneration of officials, a system of rules and files, officials are subjected to discipline and control during the performance of his duties, hierarchy, merit based selection and training[16]. The bureaucratic form according to Max Weber is the most efficient organizational form for large scale complex administration that has been developed in modern world.

In the earlier writings, Karl Marx made an attempt to conceptualize the role of bureaucracy in the corpus of state organizations while trying to develop a critique of political economy of capitalism in the nineteenth century Europe. Marx had been a keen observer and sensitive critique of contemporary European public administrative system. He observed that bureaucracy which held ultimate power and probably was not lacking in minimum good intention failed to implement remedial policies. Bureaucracy failed to dissociate itself from various aberrations because it was always conscious of promoting and safeguarding its own particular interests and did not have any surplus about projecting this as synonymous with general interest and welfare[17]. According to Marx, bureaucracy constitutes a very specific and particular social group. It is not a social class although its existence is linked to the division of society into classes. More precisely, bureaucracy as the state itself is an instrument by which the dominant class exercises its control over the other social classes. Bureaucracy does not occupy an organic position in the social structure. In the Marxian thought bureaucracy's main function is to maintain the status quo and the privileges of the master[18]. Within the broader framework of class struggle, specific instances of alienation could be found. In this process of alienation that the social forces escape from the control of man and the bureaucracy becomes an autonomous and oppressive force. Majority of the people felt that it is incompetent, mysterious and a distinct entity.

R. Michel concentrated his analysis on the internal politics of large organization and the elite domination in it. Based on his observation on the internal structure of the German Socialist Party and a series of other organizations, Michel formulated his 'Iron Law of Oligarchy' which states that modern large scale organizations by their very structure is oligarchic[19]. He concludes that all such organization tried to develop a bureaucratic structure that tried to rule out the possibility of internal democracy.

Peter Blaue describes an element of positivism when he emphasizes efficiency as the core and goal of bureaucracy. He describes bureaucrats as ritualists and explains their ritualism in terms of their fear of the superior and feeling of insecurity[20]. R. Bendix is of the view that bureaucracy is a component of an extensive social system. According to him, it is inevitable that bureaucracy is constantly affected by individuals and their views in turn vitally influencing the totality of organizational and process spheres[21]

Michel Crozier in his book "The Bureaucratic Phenomenon" suggests that bureaucracy as a part of social system, which consists of a distinctive culture, and a system of shared values[22]. V.A. Pai Panandikar and S.S. Kshir Sagar in their study of bureaucracy in India says that structural and behavioural characteristic of bureaucracy are only moderately related. The functional context of bureaucracy and the type of office and its level of mass contact to meet programmatic needs and the level of skill composition have a significant bearing on the behavioral characteristics[23]. Higher bureaucracy constitutes a small group in the government service largely drawn from members of the generalist administrative cadre. They are selected through competitive examinations after formal education. The civil servants engaged in development activities constitute the development bureaucracy[24]. The development role of higher bureaucracy can be divided into (1) policy formulation (2) advice on financial and administrative matters (3) implementation of public policies (4) training and (5) political dimensions[25].

At the level of policy formulation the political leadership in the developing countries, which took over the administration from colonial domination, is preoccupied with several problems. In many cases, political leadership lacks required experience and professional skill for development planning, thus the role of higher bureaucracy in the formulation of development policy becomes more important. In certain instances their advisory role transforms itself into the most effective factor in the determination of policies.

The higher bureaucracy has the responsibility of advising on the financial and administrative implication of decisions. This was necessitated by lack of understanding of political leadership about the intricacy and complexity of financial matters. Thus administrators have to play a crucial role in the allocation of funds for different development schemes according to priorities.

Besides the role in the policy making the higher bureaucrats are involved in implementing them and giving directions to the lower level bureaucracy as well as monitoring the implementation process. It should also be noted that after having formulated the policy, the senior bureaucrats have a very important responsibility of interpreting the policies to the lower level bureaucracy and train them in the methods to be adopted to achieve the goal. However, the political leadership in India has nurtured a different notion about the bureaucracy. By and large they regard bureaucracy as an instrument for facilitating and carrying out political dictates and it can be used for achieving their own self interests.

The top-level bureaucrats function as conveyor belt between politician and administrative machinery and thereby make political control feasible. With the task of public service being more numerous, complex and varied, there is need for competent and achievement oriented senior administrators to cope with the changing needs of the society. However, the knowledge, experience and superior skill are often not in agreement with the political leadership. They almost become integrated into political set up sharing the spoils in power. Thus they became partners in the political and administrative system.

Development Administration

The Western, especially, the American political thinkers did the conceptualization and elaboration of development administration after the Second World War. This term has been used with reference to the developing nations of Asia, Middle East and Latin America[26]. The newly liberated countries of this region were concerned with the complex process of nation-building and rapid socio-economic change. The emerging problem is how to combine skills which exist in these countries and bring them to bear more effectively in action programmes which will accelerate economic growth, expand social well being and improve public services[27].

Development in the third world became a very powerful analytical category in American social science thinking in the 1950s. It was looked at as a strategy against insurgency and growth of communism in the third world countries. The Comparative Public Administration Group in USA perceived modern administration as a mechanism for the attainment of developmental goals. To them, bureaucratization was a functional pre-requisite for maintaining stability and legitimacy in the political order. Thus bureaucracy was looked upon as a machinery for the implementation of development policies.

Development is the top priority of national governments in third world countries. Literally it means growth or improvement into a higher stage or status. It is widely conceived as a participatory process of directed social change in a society intended to bring about both social and material advancement.

Edward Weidner considers development as "a state of mind, a tendency or a direction rather than a fixed goal; it is a rate of change in a particular direction"[28]. According to John Montgomery, "development is an aspect of change that is desirable, broadly predicted or planned or influenced by governmental actions"[29]. Fred W. Riggs defines development in terms of "rising levels of autonomy or discretion in the sense of ability to choose among alternatives not of course in the sense of caution or moderation"[30].

Thus development is a process of overall change of society under mainly state directed and planned effort. In such a process of development obviously government and administrators are very much involved. The administration concerned with development activities is called development administration. It is the task of public agencies to facilitate and implement development programmes. It should be noted that development administration has grown as an academic discipline when western industrialized nations began to aid third world development through government and public institutions as agents of social change[31].

Edward Weidner has viewed development administration as the process of guiding an organization towards the achievement of progress. Political, economic and social objectives are authoritatively determined in one manner or another[32]. Development administration is the blending of all the elements and resources (human and physical) into a concerted effort to achieve agreed-upon goals. It is a continuous cycle of formulating, evaluating and implementing interrelated plan, policies, programme, projects, activities and other measures to reach established development objectives in a scheduled time sequence[33].

Development is a continuous process of formulating and implementing a set of related goals, programmes activities and tasks for achieving the stated goals in a prescribed time span. The various activities and elements that constitute the development administration are (1) formulation of development goals and policies (2) designing programme and projects as well as its management (3) reorganization of administrative structure and procedure (4) evaluation of results (5) ensuring peoples participation in development activities (6) promoting growth of social and political infrastructure (7) evaluation of results and (8) making suitable changes if needed.

Planning and coordination have become important in organizing efforts in developing countries where human and material capital are scarce and the governments are required to adopt planning for achieving socio-economic advancement. Thus development administration has become a goal-oriented endeavour. By creating and enhancing management capacities, skills and knowledge, development administration could respond to the growing needs of people. In this connection it is important to note that proper training of administrators and greater participation of the people in developmental process is a basic pre-requisite.

Another important element in development administration is creativity that means the ability and power to develop new ideas, new structures, procedures, policies, plans and programmes. In India the Integrated Rural Development Programme (IRDP), National Rural Employment Programme (NREP), Drought Prone Areas Programme (DPAP), Jawahar Rosgar Yojana (JRY) etc. are examples of such innovation for alleviation of rural poverty. It should also be noted that development administration requires an administrator who is dynamic, innovative and development-conscious to perform his role in administration. The regional diversity, ethnic composition and the reality at the grass-root level must be understood by the administrator for making the administration people- oriented[34].

Development administration assumes that bureaucracy is the most efficient and rational form of human organization. Increasing emphasis has been given to the role of bureaucrats as development administrators in charge of fostering economic growth. In developing countries bureaucracy for historical reasons is more articulated and well developed than other social structures and assumes key responsibility in socio-economic change[35]. Thus public bureaucracy retains the central place in the politico-administrative system due to its homogeneity and professional competence.

India is also strives to achieve the establishment of a developed economy, high standard of living and equal opportunity for all through democratic means. However, Indian administration still shows the continuity of the British bureaucratic tradition with its emphasis on formalism, impersonality obsession for security and lack of bureaucratic initiative. The developmental performance of India since independence suggests that our bureaucracy has neither been goal-directed nor action-directed. The Indian state and administration had failed to alleviate poverty, promote social equality and the overall development of the people.

Till the 1960s development administration was influenced by the earlier theoretical approaches to development. Development administration was supposed to be based on professionally oriented, technically competent politically and ideologically neutral bureaucratic machinery. It has to re-tool the foreign aid and also to act as the main instrument of nation building by transforming the inputs received into developmental outputs. During this period development bureaucracy was more an adaptor rather than an innovator.

But in the 1970s development could no longer be taken for granted. The western style of economic development was obviously not forthcoming; instead the quality of life of people was declining. In place of orderly change, turmoil and fragmentation proliferated throughout the country[36]. As a result in the 1980's the utility of development administration was questioned. There was an intellectual crisis set in among students of development administration. The basic contradiction that surfaced during this period was between the north and south, that is between developed and developing countries. As a result the developing countries demanded democratisation of the international political system and the creation of a "New International Economic Order". It demands for basic realignment of the world economy, through changes in trade and technological transfer was appreciated but generally ignored by the western countries[37].

It is thus clear that both internal and external forces contributed to the failure of development approach in the third world. The internal cause include traditionalism, wide spread poverty, illiteracy massive dose of political interference in the developmental initiative, inefficient and corrupt bureaucracy and the lack of adequate infrastructure to utilize natural resources. The external constraints include negative international terms of trade, the economic imperialism of multinational corporations and vulnerability and dependence of the Third World as recipients of development assistance programmes. Restrictive trade practices had the cumulative effect of leaving out in competition in the international markets.

Since 1991 the context of administration has been changing under the impact of the New Economic Policy. Concepts like Globalization, Liberalization and Privatization have gained wide currency that are indicative of more openness of government to international competition, deregulation and dismantling of series of government control and downsizing of bureaucracy by handing over selected activities to the private sector and by encouraging the non-governmental organizations to work more and more in the social development sector particularly in sectors like health, education and women's development[38]. Even the granting of aid is made conditional upon policy changes involving downsizing of the bureaucracy as well as elimination of subsidies acceptance of devaluation and other changes in the monetary and fiscal policy.

This new administrative environment, which emphasizes public-private partnership and market friendly strategies, demands a reorientation and attitudinal changes on the part of higher bureaucracy. The liberalization, privatization and globalisation would indeed pose serious challenges to the politicians and administrators to uplift their people from poverty, malnutrition, illiteracy and deprivation. In other words, the challenge before the administrators and politicians is how to achieve sustainable development through social justice and self-reliance. One of the main requirements of achieving this is the creation of a cadre of professionally trained and dedicated administrators as well as moral and just politicians who can stand against the forces of corruption and unscrupulous commercial and business interests[39]. It is clear from the above analysis that the urgent need of the developing countries is rapid social and economic change.

Socio-economic Change

Milton J. Esman defines socio-economic progress as the "sustained and widely diffused improvement in material and social welfare and nation building as the deliberate fashioning for integrated political community within fixed geographic boundaries in which the nation-state is the prominent political institution"[40].

The terms economic development, social change, nation building, modernization etc. are interchangeably used. Lack of commitment on the part of bureaucracy would be a stumbling block to administrative development. Administrative and socio-economic change with special reference to bureaucracy as an instrument of direct or planned social changes is one of the most important aspect. In almost all the planned changes, administrators are the chief implementing officers. This implies new function and challenge to bureaucracy. This new task creates new roles for bureaucrats.

Nexus between Politics and Administration

There exists the daily-lived interdependence of polity and economy between state and society and also of nations with one another. The relationship between politics and administration is well established. Politics is an activity aimed at solving the problem of human existence. Politics alone has the supreme power to transform the society to provide good life to the people. The term good life is used to denote its entire dimension. In other words politics is an activity by which society resolve public issues. Political system is a mechanism for making decision on problems affecting all or many members of the society. It is through politics that the human needs are converted into policies, which involve value system and ethical consideration. Thus politics covers all aspects of the study of governance, its structure, relationship policies and programmes[41]. Administration is the means through which the state achieves political and economic ends. The main function of political system is the formulation and the implementation of public policy through the mobilization of natural resources and their allocation for the attainment of development goals. Thus under the broad policy framework specific programme and activities are worked out by the politicians in consultation with the administrators. The administrators are to implement them for the benefit of the citizens whose name the entire government is carried out. The capacity of a political system refers to the capacity of both the policy and the government to meet heavy demands and challenges. Hence the interaction between politics and administration is of crucial importance.

Administration has some freedom of operation in its methods of working. But the scope of such freedom differs between authoritarian and democratic states[42]. In a democratic system interaction between politics and administration is inevitable. Here the political parties may come to power or go out of power but the civil servants have to carry on. The difference between politics and administration is that through politics people make social and economic choices. Administration is an instrument through which such choices are concretized[43].

Political leaders and administrators perform important function of maintaining stability, nation building and goal attainment. They constitute two fundamental instruments of social and political change. In this equilibrium sometimes the political leaders and elected representatives tend to control the administration excessively and try to bring unjust demands and pressure on administrators. They often consider bureaucracy as a tool to achieve their ends. At the same time the administrators show a tendency towards unjust compromises for their convenience. In other words both political leaders and administrators seek to exchange their power. This gives rise to tension and disputes in their interaction and does not allow them to collaborate in nation building and achieve their goals of socio-economic progress. The relation and interaction between politics and administration therefore have an important bearing on development process.

Bureaucracy and Citizen

The question naturally arises, development for whom? It is rightly said that man is the measure of everything. If the man is the central concern of development, then development administration should be people oriented. The preamble of the Indian constitution begins with

"WE, THE PEOPLE"...this means that people are supreme and administrators are the servants of the people. The term good governance denotes the quality of life of the people. Therefore, it is the supreme task of administration to formulate and implement policies, which would provide a reasonably good life for the people. In a democratic set up the satisfaction of people is the ultimate test of administration. The relation the administrators develop with the people is of considerable significance.

Administrative machinery should be extremely sensitive to popular demands. But quite often administrative practice does not infuse confidence in public. The Indian administrative system has not shown much evidence of mobility and flexibility. Often there is manifest tendency on the part of bureaucrats to divert themselves from the mainstream. Obsession with rules rather than concern for output, delays and mediocrity at all levels are some of the factors inhibiting output of the government.

In a welfare setup public becomes increasingly the owner beneficiary of governmental programmes. The extension of governmental responsibility over a wide field of activities does not necessarily means that government is very popular in the eyes of the people. There is wide spread feeling among the citizens that, the administration has not come up with the expectations of the welfare state, and its performance in dealing with citizens comes much to be desired. Over the years bureaucracy has become insensitive and even hostile to the poor sections. Even the senior officers seem to be apathetic towards them.

An important development in the last twelve years has been a change in the economic policy of the government, towards reducing the governmental control and encouraging free market. The government system is gradually reducing to a non-performing entity. Here the benefits of the poor have been so far marginal and the impact of the reform on the poor has been adverse because of their vulnerable socio-economic position. The development schemes aimed at improving their bargaining power are a big failure. The sociological and political factors that lie behind the institutional constraints on poverty reduction get little mention in the government programmes. Bureaucracy, basically due to indifference is totally out of touch with this problem. Here the most prominent trend in these years is increasing corruption, declining performance and lack of concern for the poor[44].

References

1. Hahn-Been Lee, "The Role of Higher Civil Service Under Rapid Social and Political Change" in Edward W. Weidner (ed.), *Development Administration in Asia* Durham: Duke University Press, 1970, p. 108.
2. R.B. Jain, *Public Administration in India in the 21st Century Challenges for Good Governance*, New Delhi: Deep & Deep Publications, 2002, p.150.

Also see R. Dwarakadas, *Role of Civil Service in India*, Bombay: Popular Book Depot, 1958.

3. *Ibid.*
4. Rumki Basu, *Introduction to Public Administration*, New Delhi: Sterling Publishers, 1991, p.57.
5. R.B. Jain, *op. cit.*, p.151.
6. For more details see

   (1) B.B. Mishra, *The Bureaucracy in India. A Historical Analysis of Development up to 1947,* New Delhi: Oxford University Press, 1977.

   (2) Sapru, R.K. *Civil Service Administration in India,* New Delhi: Deep & Deep Publications, 1985.
7. Premlatha Bansal, *Administrative Development in India*, New Delhi: Sterling Publishers, 1974, p.11.
8. R.B. Jain, *op. cit.*, p.152.
9. P.C. Alexander, "Civil Service: Continuity and Change" in Hiranmay Karlekar (ed.) *Independent India- The First Fifty Years*, New Delhi: Indian Council for Cultural Relations, 1998, p. 60.
10. Lata Sinha, "Role and Rationale of All India Service", *Indian Journal of Public Administration*, Vol. XXXVI. No. 4 October-December, 1990, p. 814.
11. B.M. Verma, *Welfare Measures for Weaker Sections- A Policy Analysis*, New Delhi: Devaki Publications, 1996, p.198.
12. K. Sukumaran Nair, *Administrative Co-ordination at State Level in India – A Study of Government Secretariat and the Board of Revenue in Kerala*, Thiruvananthapuram: Kerala Academy of Political Science, 1975, p. XV.
13. R.K. Suresh Kumar, "Combating Administrative Inefficiency in Kerala- Revamping the Second Layer of Administration", *ISDA Journal*, Vol. 4, Nos. 3 & 4, July – December 1999, p.246.
14. M.G. Ramakant Rao and Prashant K. Mathur, *Advanced Public Administration- Policy, Planning and Decision Making,*Vol. 2, New Delhi: Kanishka Publishers, 1994, p.46.
15. *Ibid.*
16. Max Weber, *The Theory of Social and Economic Organisation*, New York: Oxford University Press, 1947, pp. 333-334.

    (Also see) Joseph La Palombara (ed.), *Bureaucracy and Political Development*, New Jersey: Princeton University Press, 1963.
17. V.A. Pai Panandikar and S.S. Kshir Sagar, *Bureaucracy and Development Administration*, New Delhi: Centre for Policy Research, 1978, p. 6.

18. V.A. Pai Panandikar, R.N. Bishnoi, O.P. Sharma, *Development Bureaucracy*, New Delhi: Oxford & IBH Publishing Co., 1983, p. 2.
19. R. Michel, *Political Parties: A Sociological Study of the Oligarchical Tendencies of Modern Democracy*, New York: Dover Publishers, 1954, Chapter 1-5.
20. Peter Blaue, *Bureaucracy in Modern Society*, New York: Random House, 1965, pp. 50-52.
21. R. Bendix, "Bureaucracy", *International Encyclopedia of Social Science*, New York: MacMillan, 1959, p. 2006.
22. Michel Crozier, *The Bureaucratic Phenomenon*, Chicago: University of Chicago Press, 1964, p.320.
23. V.A. Pai Panandikar and Kshir Sagar, *op. cit.*, p.6.
24. Victor A. Thompson, "Administrative Objection for Development Administration," *Administrative Science Quarterly*, Vol. 9, June 1964, p.91.
25. R.K. Sapru, *Development Administration*, New Delhi: Deep & Deep Publications, 1994. pp. 276-278.
26. O.P. Dwivedi, *Development Administration: From Underdevelopment to Sustainable Development*, London: MacMillan Press, 1994, pp. 1-3.
27. Milton J. Esman and John D. Montgomery, "System Approaches to Technical Cooperation: The Role of Developmental Administration", *Public Administration Review*, Vol. 29, No.5, September- October 1969, p. 508.
28. Edward W. Weidner, "The Elements of Development Administration" in Edward Weidner (ed.) *Development Administration in Asia, op. cit.*, p.8.
29. John Montgomery, "A Royal Invitation: Variation on Three Classic Themes" in Montgomery and William Siffin (eds.) *Approaches to Development: Politics, Administration and Change*, New York: Mc Graw-Hill, 1966, p. 59.
30. Fred W. Riggs, "The Idea of Development Administration" in Edward W. Weidner (ed.) *op. cit.*, p. 27.
31. O.P. Dwivedi, "Development Administration: An Overview" in T.N. Chaturvedi (ed.), *Fifty Years of Indian Administration Retrospect and Prospects*, New Delhi: Indian Institute of Public Administration, 1998, pp. 48-49.
32. Edward W. Weidner, *op. cit.*, p. 399.
33. Donald C. Stone, "Tasks, Precedents and Approaches to Education and Development Administration" in Donald C. Stone

(ed.), *Education for Development Administration*, Brussels: International Institute of Administrative Sciences, 1966, p. 41.

34. R.K Sapru, *op. cit.*, pp. 125-129.
35. C.P. Bhambhri, "Bureaucracy in India: Challenges of the Eighties" *Indian Journal of Public Administration*, Vol. XXVI, No.3, July- September 1980, p. 520.
36. O.P. Dwivedi, *op. cit.*, p. 53.
37. *Ibid.*
38. Mohit Bhattacharya, "Public Administration Today and Tomorrow" in T.N. Chaturvedi (ed.), *Fifty Years of Indian Administration*, *op. cit.*, p. 62.
39. O.P. Dwivedi, *op. cit.*, p. 62.
40. Milton J. Esman, cited by John Montgomery and William Siffin (eds.) *op. cit.*, pp. 59-60.
41. T.N. Dhar, "Government and Administration" in *Third World Issues*, New Delhi: Indian Institute of Public Administration, 1983, p. 4.
42. S.R. Maheswari, *Comparative Government and Politics*, Agra: Lakshmi Narayan Agarwal Educational Publication, 1983, p. 3.
43. T.N. Dhar, *op. cit.*, p. 4.
44. N.C. Saxena, *op. cit.*, p. 5.

2

Socio-Economic and Political Milieu of Kerala

The study of higher bureaucracy will not be complete with out an understanding off the socio-economic and political context where it operates. Bureaucracy is the part of legal political superstructure, which is largely conditioned by the socio-economic structure of the society. This is because the administration in a society functions as an integral part of the larger socio-political system. Therefore, it must be noted that the character of the society affects the nature and functioning of the bureaucracy. It should also be pointed out that the civil servants are the recently urbanized strata of the rich and influential section of the society. The bureaucracy and the political leadership have a similar socio-economic background. This becomes explicit in the context of Kerala where there is no wide rural urban divide. Even the non- Kerala civil servants and their background are similar to that of Kerala.

The state of Kerala as a political unit came in to existence on November 1, 1956 by integrating the Malayalam speaking former princely states of Travancore and Cochin with the Malabar districts of the former British colonial province of Madras. Before the formation of Kerala, these princely states differ in their administrative structure and institutions. The state is situated at the south-western corner of India. It has a geographical area of about 38863 sq. km. and has long coastal line. The area of the state work out to be 1.18 percent of the total area of the country. According to 2001 census the total population of Kerala state is 31838619, which comprises of 15468664 males and 16369955 females[1]. The state leads rest of India in the case of literacy. The rate of literacy is 90.92 percent with a break up of 94.20 percent for male and 87.86 percent for female. The density of population is 819 persons per sq. km. Kerala is in third position in respect of density. The first position is being occupied by West Bengal and second by Bihar. The sex ratio is 1058 females per 1000 males[2].

The progress and development of a country depends upon the efficiency of its administrative set up. The civil service comprising officers of various grades carries out the day-to-day administration of the government. The top civil servant who usually belongs to the Indian Administrative Service is secretary to government in each department. These officers are entrusted with the overall supervision and direction of the department administration. Outside the ministries but subject to the control and supervision of the ministers there are a number of semi-autonomous enterprises like corporations and boards. Such enterprises are usually manned by officers belong to Indian Administrative Service. For administrative convenience the state is divided in to 14 districts. The districts is further divided into Taluks. District collector who is usually an IAS officer heads the district. The district collector is entrusted with a wide range of powers and functions. He is in charge of revenue administration and maintenance of law and order. Collector is in charge of Development Administration of the districts.

The officers implement the policies of the government. So the development of a country is very much depending upon the efficiency and effectiveness of its civil service. Maintenance of efficiency requires adequate planning based on administrative thinking. Here the most important one is the ability and competence of the higher bureaucracy who is at the upper strata of the administrative structure belongs to the Indian Administrative Service. These officers are relatively permanent top group of civil servants who are placed between the political decision makers and the rank and file bureaucracy. These officers share in different degrees the task of directing the various administrative agencies.

After independence the state has been embarking upon national plans and programmes for accelerating the pace of economic and social development. Kerala is the first state, which voted against the congress party and brought communist party into power. The first democratically elected communist government was different from the earlier government, because the state power was used as an instrument for bringing about development and radical socio-economic changes[3]. This was because of the commitment of the communist party for radical restructuring of Kerala society within the limitation of the Indian legal constitutional framework. The first Chief Minister E.M.S. Namboothiripad was the most prominent Marxian theoretician and has played an important role in the socio political and cultural life of Kerala[4].

With a short span of 45 years Kerala state had made remarkable achievements in almost every field. According to Amartya Sen, despite the fact that economic growth in Kerala has been slow but it has achieved tremendous results in important areas such as literacy, life expectancy and mortality rates[5] Kerala has showed the world that economic growth is not a pre requisite for development. This is because of its achievements in respect of basic educational health and demographic achievements are far ahead of the rest of India. Kerala rates fifth among major states with regard to growth rate of states income. The growth rate of 59.8 percent achieved by Kerala during the period of 1989-90 to 1997-1998 is higher than that of Tamil Nadu with 58.64 percent and Karnataka with 51.64 percent.

According to Amartya Sen, India does not need to look elsewhere for development pointers. Yet there is much that India can learn from Kerala's development experience[6]. From an international developmental perspective Kerala's position is comparable or and is better than countries like Srilanka, Cuba, Costa-Rica etc. where development is synonymous with economic development. Kerala's achievements in all these areas are within the framework of parliamentary democracy. The reasons for these achievements are many such as socio-religious, political and administrative factors.

Social Aspects

In the social field the state resolved the first generation problem like illiteracy high infant mortality rate, high maternal mortality rate, low expectation of life at the time of birth and related indication of under development. Kerala has a high human development index despite low per capita income compared to Punjab[7].

A high degree of progress is achieved by the state in the field of education. It is not because of planning alone but many years of dedicated work from the part of state and private agencies. Among the various factors responsible for education most important were progressive steps taken by the enlightened rulers of Travanvcore and Cochin.

Kerala is the first state in India implemented free and compulsory education in primary classes. The liberal educational policy of the democratic governments and the special interest taken by different communities like Christian Missionaries helped to a very great extend[8]. Government is spending a good share of its income to the expansion of educational activities. The communist coalition government of E.K. Nayanar (1987-1991) provided administrative and institutional support to the Total Literacy Programme[9].

The students belong to SC/ST and backward classes and economically backward communities are exempted from payment of fees at all levels of education. The SC/ST students are eligible for lump-sum grant to meet their educational expenses. A policy was maintained for them for reservation of seats in educational institutions including professional colleges[10].

Kerala has achieved near equality in school enrolment in terms of gender. The girl students enrolment is 49..1 percent. The all India average is only 39 percent. The enrolment of SC/ST students in schools is 11.77 percent of the total school enrolment. 43.3 percent of the SC/ST students studies in government schools and 55.5 percent students studies in private aided schools and 11.2 percent in private unaided school[11]. During the past decades Kerala's expenditure on education ranged from 30 to 40 percent of the total revenue receipts. The total expenditure on education during 1999-2000 stood at Rs.2481 crore of which primary education accounted for 50 percent, secondary education 31 percent and university and higher education 14 percent.

Primary and secondary school education has been a success in promoting general literacy and quality of life. But higher education tells a very different story because Kerala has the worst record of educated unemployment in the country and probably in the world. A peculiar feature of Kerala's unemployment is that the job seekers are graduates and post-graduates[12].

The quality of higher education has deteriorated and students are ill equipped to compete in national competitive examinations especially civil service. Kerala shows an inverse relationship between growth in education and economic development. Those who are concerned with higher education – politicians, bureaucrats and academicians are not interested to take any radical steps to solve these problems.

Health

In Kerala, the government has for a long time adopted all possible measures to raise the general standard of health of the population. The history of modern medical and public health in the states back to the 19th century. They opened several hospitals and took personal interest in adopting western medicine and surgery. In addition the government introduced a system of grants to private medical institutions. Kerala has the lowest birth and death rate in India and has more hospital beds in relation to the population than any other state. Kerala's success in improving health conditions of the people in a short span was due to the policies which successive governments in Kerala followed since independence. Kerala has already attained high health standards in respect of all standard indication of maternal, infant, child health as well as general health of the population. Kerala's achievement is at par with high human development as classified in the Human Development Report 1998 (UNDP 1998, p.1448). Infant mortality rate in Kerala is 1.56 percent (India 7.16%) and child mortality rate in Kerala is 0.46 percent (India 2.63%)[13]. Kerala has almost attained universalisation of immunization. Higher level of education especially female education and improved health care infrastructure are some of the reason for this and in Kerala income is not a major criterion for this[14]. In Kerala health care system is available not only in urban areas but also in rural areas too. Together with government sector, the private sector also played a key role in such a high standard. The percapita expenditure in current prices in health including family welfare by the state government has become five times what it was in 1985-86. It was doubled between 1994-1995 and 1999-2000[15].

Like education critics have been expressing their distress over the health care system also. The medical system is becoming more and more commercialised and market oriented. The relation between doctor and patient is rigid. The health status in Kerala has emerged as a low mortality high morbidity syndrome. As for the morbidity pattern, the diseases of poverty seem to co-exist with the so-called disease of affluence. In the changing new world order, the state government is increased the fees and charge of government hospitals and it is reported that government is planning to privatise medical institutions.

Public Distribution System

The public distribution system in Kerala occupies an important place in the welfare programmes of the state government. The public distribution system was first established during the Second World War when the state experienced acute food shortage. Due to the pressure from various organizations like Trade Union, Peasant Organization and of the administrative needs of the British government itself, ration shops were set up[16]. An attempt to establish an extensive public food distribution system of permanent nature in the state began with the first Communist Ministry of 1957. It was only in the mid 1970's that the quantity of commodities distributed could be increased[17].

The public distribution system was established and strengthened in Kerala in 1970's and 1980s. The public distribution of food takes place in Kerala at the primary school level up to 10 years old children and for general public on controlled prices through ration shops. Even though PDS is a comprehensive scheme at school level only ¾ of primary school children are availing this facility[18]. Through the fair price shops, provide food grains and certain essential commodities like sugar, wheat edible oils etc. at controlled prices. The PDS reaches out to the remote villages of the state and with the help of this the poor particularly the landless in rural areas are able to be fed. Civil supplies corporation in collaboration with co-operative societies and by timely intervention in the market through its retail Maveli shops distribute essential commodities in reasonable prices.

In addition to this, other forms of PDS also operate within the state in maternity and child health programmes. Here food is distributed as a supplementary nutrition programme for pregnant mother and pre-school children of poorer households through *Balawadis, Anganwadis* and *Mahila Samajams*[19].

Recently the government of India decided to restrict PDS supply of rice at concessional rates to only 25 percent of population falling below the poverty line. However, the state government extended the benefits to 42 percent[20]. The frequent increase of prices of essential commodities through ration shops by the central government is also a threat to the public distribution system of food.

Economically Kerala is one of the less developed states in India. It ranks fifth in term of growth rate. The lack of major industries, mineral wealth, unemployment, over population are some of the problems faced by the state. Basically Kerala's problem is that it does not and cannot generate enough revenue to finance and maintain its social development, which results increasing budget deficit[21]. The deficit is largely in the revenue account that finance current consumption. The government has been attempting to finance their deficit by using capital receipt and public accounts. This severely reduces the government's ability to incur capital expenditures. Secondly, the revenue expenditures are inherently liable to increase over the years because inflation and second-generation requirements of social developments. For instance, expenditure on health care and pension payments have been going up as the increase in life expectancy has been significant. At the same time Kerala government's ability to raise resources is severely constrained by reasons such as stagnation in the tax base and control of taxation policy by the central government e.g. the state government has no control over gulf remittance. The public sector undertakings has been unable to obtain its fair share of central government transfers which are distributed according to rules and priorities that do not takes into account the specific nature of Kerala's problems. For example, Kerala does not receive its share for social development since it is seen as having reached the national targets despite the fact that the state is unable to meet the recurring expenditures needed to sustain these achievements[22].

The economy of Kerala is agriculture based. Due to historical and climatic reasons the state has developed cash crops rather than food grains. Kerala's economy during the past few years has been passing through difficult condition largely due to fall in prices of principal agricultural commodities such as coconut, cardamom, pepper, tea, coffee etc[23]. There was a decline in the output for paddy, tapioca, banana, coconut, cashew, and arecanut. So the state is heavily dependent upon other states for food grains and other essential commodities. The only major crop that showed an increase in output was rubber. The major section of the state's working population depends upon agriculture for livelihood. The liberalization policies of the Government of India have substantially subdued the agrarian economy of the state. The production of agriculture food grain continued to be very low, just 38 kg compared to 203 kg of all India[24].

Now agriculture is neither a subsistence activity nor a viable economic enterprise except for a limited number of plantation crops. The increase in price of land has little to do with their value for agriculture, land is real estate, needed for residence and status and also generally seen as the safest and best investment. The increasing migration rate to Gulf countries is also one of the reasons for raising the cost of land[25]. This has lead to a radical transformation in the nature of agricultural activities, unemployment and lifestyle. Second a substantial number of agricultural families have non-agricultural source of income mainly remittances in the service sector of Kerala. Next, a variety of traditional economic activities including the cultivation of many seasonal crops and many small business are no longer seen as economically viable. There is co-existence of labour shortage with high unemployment levels partly because these jobs are not white-collar jobs. Kerala economy exists and functions as an integral part of the Indian economy and policy and the under development periphery of a world economic system[26].

Compared to many other states, Kerala has several advantages, which would contribute to a strong industrial base. The state has abundant potential for hydro electric power, excellent road and water transport facilities, some of the world's rarest minerals like illminite and monazite, a large coastal area for fish landing, very rich forest resources and the most literate people[27]. Yet Kerala remain industrially backward. A high portion of the states working force is employed in low productivity agro-based traditional and backward industries such as coir, cashew, handloom and beedi etc. As a result the average earnings per industrial workers in Kerala is about half of the national wage level[28]. Even though the state has abundant potential for hydroelectric resources the power shortage is a serious handicap to the industrialization of the state. Now both the central and state governments are planning to leave the power projects to the private sector including multinational companies. The recent manpower export to the Gulf countries and the brain drain to western countries have severely affected the economic and social balance among the people of the state. The migrants were accused of wasting hard earned money in non-productive investments like houses. This exposed the people to the western style of living along with providing several families with the required purchasing power to pursue such a life style[29]. The electronic and print machines have a large impact on the life of the people. The NRI of Kerala has also failed to make productive investment in the state.

The Kerala labour which has evolved in a difficult development legacy with great right consciousness, non-feudal relations of production, egalitarian cultural ethics, emphasis on human dignity may come to be regarded as militant by the capitalist classes within the state and outside the state are some of the reasons for lack of industrialization. For such class-consciousness, the reform movements of the various religious and political organization paved the way for the lower caste people to the mainstream of the society.

Socio Religious Movements

Kerala society is multi religious. The Hindus, Christians and Muslims are the three major religions. The followers of other religions are comparatively negligible. The caste is a dominant factor in the life of the people. This caused the division of the society especially among Hindus and even denial of basic human rights to the majority of Hindus. The four major communities are Ezhava, Nair, Christians and Muslims. These communities having more or less equal strength are exerting pressure on Kerala politics. The class interest of these communities creates problems in the political and administrative scene of Kerala.

During the first five centuries after Christ several Kingdoms were developed known as Sangham Age. The region has a long history of communal and cultural contacts with Arabs, Greeks, Romans and Chinese traders. Several world religions like Buddhism, Jainism, Hinduism, Islam, Christianity, Judaism etc were existed here[30]. In the third century there existed Jainism in the region and Buddhism followed it. Until eighth century Kerala was a Buddhist country and the society was egalitarian[31]. The components of caste system were assimilated into the Kerala society from the north between seventh and eighth centuries. About this time the present day Brahmin elite caste took the hold. They have gradually won over the Chieftains of various principalities ordaining them to be Kshatriyas by elaborate and impressive rituals and extending justification for every action[32].

In 1498 Portuguese arrived in Calicut for trade followed by Dutch, British and French. Kerala's natural resources and commercial nature of its agricultural crops attracted the foreign traders[33]. In 1792 the English effectively took power. Throughout the nineteenth and twentieth century British governed this region.

Christianity is said to be introduced into Kerala by the year 52 AD by St.Thomas. The powerful caste system of Hindu society penetrated into Christian society also. The growth of trade and spread of Islam were parallel. Large scale conversion was aided by the invasion of Tippu Sultan.

By the beginning of the seventeenth century caste hierarchy and Brahmin's supremacy were relatively well established in Kerala. The Malayali Brahmins known as Namboothiris and the ruling elite known as Kshatriyas established their authority over land and from the princinetes of the temples. As the need for services increased, more and more people were recruited and were known as '*Sudras*' of various grades[34]. By the wake of nineteenth century there were 96 groups of various grades and differing status. All the four Varnas were gradually transplanted to Kerala. As the caste system advance in Kerala the entire society was infinitely fragmented and malicious form of untouchabilility was practiced

The society was not based on the principle of social freedom and equality. The rigid caste system and irrational caste taboos existed. The lower orders were not only untouchables but also unapproachable[35]. They were denied entry to temples and admission to schools, colleges and public services. The upper castes like the Namboothiris, Kshathriyas, Nairs etc. enjoyed several immunities and privileges[36]. The law that prevailed in land was not egalitarian.

This inequality and religious rivalry paved the way for social reform movement in Kerala and this movement have a greater impact on its politics and administration. There were caste based movements among many communities. The most important reforms were among the Ezhavas, Nairs and Pulayas.

The reform movement among the Ezhavas was lead by Sree Narayana Guru a religious scholar, philosopher, saint and social reformer. Guru criticized and campaigned against the evils of caste system. The movement took into an organized form in 1903, known as Sree Narayana Dharmma Paripalana Yogam or SNDP[37]. The major supporters of these movements were Dr. Palpu and Kumaranasan. The major activity of the movement was securing of constitutional rights and establishment of educational institutions[38].

The movement influenced not only the members of the Ezhava community but the Nair community also took to such activities on community basis. Chattampi Swamikal established a good rapport with Sree Narayana Guru and they together worked for the cuase of Hindu social and moral regeneration. With the aim of reforming Nair community and abolishing social evils formed an orgnisation known as Nair Service Society in 1914. The NSS in course of time developed into a powerful organization[39]. The reform movement of SNDP yogam inspired the Pulayas, the landless agriculture labouring caste and their leader Ayyankali to initiate organizational work among them. They expressed the need for education of the members of the community, self respect and fight for the rights that had been denied for them so far.

The Namboothiris started Yogakshema Sabha in 1908 with the objective of eradicating the evil social customs and ensuring the all round progress of the community. The minority communities like the Christians and Muslims were also influenced by the social reform movements among the Hindus and organized themselves for the social and economic uplift of their community.

As a result of various social reform movements, the obsolete custom prevailing among various castes and communities were steadily given up and people developed a modern and progressive outlook[40]. The need to break away from the restraints of caste was felt by more radical elements with the social reform movement[41]. The radical political element first emerged as Leftist and the group quickly turned into communist organization. It is this movement that was more successful than any other movement in mobilizing the labouring poor and calling crossing caste identities[42]. The underprivileged sections of society who had been subjected to social disabilities over centuries become conscious of their rights as well as their strength. In such circumstances the demand for land reform grow in momentum among the tenants.

Land Reform

The history of land struggle in Kerala is very complex. The land monopoly had been the result of feudalist structure of pre-colonial agrarian relation. The land was the major source of wealth. The poor farmers worked in this land of the feudals for their lively hood.

One of the earliest pieces of land legislation in Travancore was the *'Pattam'* Proclamation of 1865[43]. It enfranchised *'Sirkar Pattam'* lands conferring proprietary rights on the holders of *Pandaravaka* (*sirkar*) land and protected the tenants from the fear of arbitrary eviction. The Royal Proclamation of 1867, which defined the rights and obligation of tenants and landlords. The proclamation was codified as the *Jenmi-*

Kudyian Regulation and later it was amended in 1932. Which conferred full proprietary rights on *Kudiyan* subjected to the payment of *Jenmikaram.*

The land reform in Cochin was to prevent eviction and to give permanent rights to the tenants. The Royal writ issued in 1863 prevented eviction of '*Kanam*' tenants before a period of 12 years. The Tenancy Act of 1915 granted fixity of tenure to those who took *Kanam* holdings before 1888 and to provide for payment of compensation to tenants for the improvements effected by them. The Cochin Tenancy Act passed in 1938 conferred security of tenure on '*Kanam*' created between 1885 and 1915 and imposed further restrictions on eviction of tenants. The *Verum Pattamdar* Act of 1943, protected the interest of the tenants at will and granted security of tenure to leases and subleases in respect of their holdings[44].

Malabar had the greatest struggle over land rights. The Malabar Compensation for Tenants Improvement Act passed in 1887 was to prevent the growing practice of eviction. This Act was amended in 1900 to rectify its defects but eviction continued still a large scale. In 1930 the Malabar Tenancy Act passed. It contained elaborate provision to confer security of tenure on several categories of tenants and to enable the aggrieved party to have the fair rent fixed by civil courts. This Act was amended in 1945,1951 and 1954 to satisfy the interest of the tenants.

After independence, the Travancore-Cochin government passed the Stay of Eviction Proceedings, Act in 1950 to give protection of the *'ryots'* from arbitrary eviction[45]. The first communist ministry of 1957 passed a series of four major land reform laws. In 1962 this was struck by the High Court of Kerala, subsequently in 1963 the Kerala Land Reform Act was passed. This Act bans the creation of fresh tenancies, confers on the tenants the right to purchase his owners land and presents a ceiling in regard to the extent of land that can be owned by a family. This act was amended in 1969, it abolished Jenmi system in Kerala and confers full right of ownership to the tillers of the soil[46]. The 1969 land reform is considered as one of the most radical and most successful in south Asia.

These Land Acts were not the out come of merely through a vote in the legislature. It was the result of decades of organizing, petition signing, marching, meeting, strikes, battles with police and landlords, election campaign and parliamentary debates[47]. Thus the series of land reform introduced in Kerala since the latter half of the 19th century has helped in accelerating the social economic and educational progress of the state. Even though land reform in Kerala did not transfer agrarian power to agricultural labourers and poor peasants and end capitalist landlords, it was able to abolish Jenmi system and the concentration of ownership of landlords and weakened Nair landlordism. At the same time landless labour households were able to improve their bargaining powers in the labour market, and the agricultural workers made the real wage gainers through the Land Reform Act. It helped in establishing a more egalitarian rural society[48]. Compared to other states, in Kerala the wage rate of agriculture workers have increased.

Apart from land reforms, Kerala government has taken initiative in the field of labour legislation and welfare. The government also took initiative to a number of poverty alleviation programmes, granting of old age pension to rural workers, unemployment wages, widow pension and the implementation of national programmes of poverty alleviation such as IRDP and the allied programmes[49].

Administrative History

Travancore

During the *Shangham* period government was vested in a hierarchical council formed of Brahmins of the *Sixty Four Grammas*, or villages[50]. The Brahmins rented the land to the inhabitants of the country recovering their right of property and management of public affairs. The defence of the country and the use of weapons were entrusted to ten divisions and a half out of the *Sixty Four Gramas*. The executive government was consigned to one person and a council of four others appointed by the Brahmins of these villages for three years. This led to the origin of customs of rotation of rulers[51]. In every twelve years the ruler was changed. These arrangements in the course of time might have lead to the election of one ruler of the military caste who took an oath on assumption of office to acknowledge the authority of the Brahmins and do nothing against their interests. By about eighth century the influence of Brahmins and the prosperity of their colonies passed the way for social, cultural and political separation of Kerala from the Tamil country. In due course, the whole of Kerala came to be covered by a network of temple centered Brahmin settlement

The end of Chera reign was followed by a division of the country among local ruling chieftains. The conflicts and feuds of this local chieftains lead to the invasion of Muslims and later the consolidation of power in the hands of foreigners. The lineal descendents of the last perumal was the Raja of Cochin. The two other superior chieftains were the Maharaja of Travancore and the Zamoorins of Calicut[52].

The organizations such as *Three hundred, Five hundred, Six hundred* and *Five thousands* which check the despotism of the local rulers and preserved the right and privileges of the people[53]. The state was divided in to several *Nadus* under the local chieftains called the *Desavazhi* who were responsible to the King. Each *Nadu* consisted of *Desham, Kara, Thara, Cheries* or other similar divisions. The popular assemblies in these divisions and sub divisions are called *Koottams.* The *Koottam* played a significant role in arousing public opinion against the unilateral and autocratic acts of the rulers in local issues. The *Brahmin and Nair* aristocracy dominates the *Koottams.* This functioned actively in ancient and medieval Kerala till the collapse of the self sufficient economy under the impact of the British domination[54].

By the 12th century, Venad became the most powerful princely Kingdom of the southern most part. Later it came to be known as Travancore and its capital was Kollam. The King was the fountainhead of the executive authority in Travancore. The chief executive officer was the "*Valiakariakar*"[55]. The region was divided into district, sub district or village, which was governed by local chiefs. In 1684 Ravi Varma ascended to the throne and effected changes in the administrative setup. All the administrative business was transacted only after obtaining royal sanction and the post of *Valiakariakar* was replaced by *Valiasarvadhikariakar.* When Marthanda Varma became the king in 1729, radically reorganized the internal administration[56]. The lowest unit, village was put under *Pravarthikar.* A group of village constituted the *Mandapathum Vathukkal* which was put under *Kariakar* (Thahasildhar). The chief executive officer *Valiasarvadhikariakar* was replaced by *Dalwa.* During the reign of Dharma Raja, *Dalwa* was renamed as *Diwan*[57].

A formal treaty was concluded between Travancore and English East India Company in 1795 on the basis of these Travancore rulers accepted British supremacy and the company promised to help the state in the event of external aggression. Under the new treaty concluded in 1805 Travancore became the subsidiary ally of the British and accepted British protection. This led to the practice of appointment of *Diwan* with the concurrence of the British Residents. The King issued *Chattavariolas* containing rules of conduct for the officers of the state. The *Diwan* was the chief executive officer who with a great body of officials conducted the administration.

Under the reign of Dharma Raja, Travancore was divided in to three provinces viz. northern, southern and western and each of which was placed under *Valiasarvadhikariakar*. It was further divided into Taluks under S*arvadhikariakar*. It was again divided and placed *Kariakar, Manian, Kelvies, Adhikaram and Provarthies* were small units under the charge of *Manikaran, Adhikari and Provartikar*. They were assisted by Writers, Accountants, *Rayasar* and *Sepoys*[58].

Col. Munro (1806-1818) who became the Resident cum *Diwan* of Travancore subsequently built up a centralized administration. He reorganised the entire administrative machinery similar to Madras presidency. In the year 1835 the state was divided into two revenue divisions, the southern and northern and each was placed under the charge of *Diwan Peishkar* equivalent to the collector in British provinces. The head of the taluk was *Thahasildar*. Between *Peishkar* and *Thahasildar* there existed an *Assistant Peishkar*[59]. The entire revenue administration was under the overall leadership of the *Diwan Peishkar* who enjoyed a higher defacto status. At the close of the 19th century there were four divisions, 32 taluks and 422 *pakuthis*[60]. In between 1911 and 1921 the number of administrative divisions reduced to 4 and the taluks to 30. During 1921-41, the territorial units underwent several changes and during the period of 1941 census the number of administrative divisions consisted of three revenue divisions 30 taluks and 484 pakuthis. Of the 30 taluks, 15 taluks had been grouped under 7 revenue sub divisions each in charge of an *Assistant Peishkar*[61]. This was the position of the state of Travancore at the time of independence.

Col. Munro also introduced the British model modern secretariat in Travancore. He introduced administration conducted by the *Diwan* from the head quarters, assisted by the subordinate staff such as *Diwan Peishkar*. He organized separate department headed by persons who simultaneously discharged their duties and to act as a check up on each other and introduced office procedure[62]. Diwan T. Madhava Rao made certain important changes in the secretariat. He reshuffled the whole system of administration[63]. One chief secretary to Government was appointed.

In 1920 the secretariat was reorganized on the basis of recommendations of salary committee[64]. Through this reorganization the secretariat came under the sole control of the chief secretary. Later important changes in the secretariat were made by Sree Chithira Thirunal Maharaja, who appointed Sir. C.P. Ramaswamy Iyer as *Diwan* in 1936. In 1944 the secretariat consisted of two parts, the general and the revenue. The administration of the general and revenue secretariat was conducted by a superior staff of officers assisted by ministerial staff and clerks. The superior staff consisted of 3 secretaries and 6 assistant secretaries. The *Diwan* had one private secretary and one administrative secretary. This system continued till independence[65].

At the time of integration of Travancore and Cochin the superior staff of the Travancore secretariat consisted of one chief secretary, six secretaries and one head translator. The work of all secretaries was concretized through the chief secretary who did not hold charge of any separate department.

The first Legislative Council in Travancore was established in 1888, which consisted of 5 officials and 3 nominated non-official members with *Diwan* as the president. For giving more popular base, Sree Moolam Popular Assembly was created in 1904[66]. The freedom of speech was granted to the Assembly. By the Act of 1922, membership was raised to fifty of which 28 were elected non-official, and the right to stand election and the right to vote were extended to women also. The Reform Act of 1932 gave it a statutory base and changed the Assembly into a bicameral legislature known as Sree Chitra State Council and Sree Moolam Assembly. The Assembly consisted of 72 members and had the right to elect a Deputy President. The Act of 1947 further modified the bicameral legislature, the election to upper chamber was on adult franchise. The chief executive was *Diwan*, he was not responsible to the legislature. The system continued till independence.

Cochin

According to the tradition, the Raja of Cochin claimed to hold the territory in the right to descend from Cheraman Perumal, who governed the whole provinces of Kerala including Travancore and Cochin. In the central province, the dynasty that ruled was called *Perumpadappu Swaroopam.* Upto1500 AD Cochin was only a small principality[67]. The king was the supreme head of administration.

Like the rest of Kerala the kingdom was divided into a number of Nadu's or districts, each of which was under the control of *Naduvazhi.* Each *Nadu* was divided into caste or tribal group rather than territorial units. The caste groups are known as the *Gramas* of the *Namboothiri's*, the *Thara* of the Nairs and *Cherry* of the lower castes[68].

The *Desam* was ruled by *Desavazhi*, who was responsible for the execution of all the orders of the king.

By the end of the 16th century Cochin acquired more territories with the help of Portuguese. In 1759 this was attacked by the Zamoorins of Calicut who was expelled by the Raja of Travancore. As a reward certain provinces were transferred to Travancore in 1761. After this treaty the king, Kerala Varma introduced a new system of administration in Cochin. The *Nadu* or district were renamed as *Kovilakathum Vathukal* or Taluks and it was placed under *Karyakar*, who enjoyed both judicial and executive powers. The Taluks were again divided into *Provarties* which formed the unit of administration. The *Provarties* were presided over by *Provartikarans* assisted by Menons or Accountants and *Chandrakarans* or Cash keepers. The Taluks were grouped into two divisions each under *Sarvadhikaryakar*. The head of administration was *Valiasarvadhikariakar* or Prime Minister who was also the head of the army.

By a treaty concluded in 1791 Cochin became the vassal of English East India Company, paying annual tribute to the company. During this time Col. Munro became the Resident *Diwan* of Cochin[69]. *Diwan* was the head of the revenue department and exercised magisterial function. The secretariat system was organized in Cochin in 1895 according to the model of British secretariat system. The chief executive officer, the *Diwan* was the channel of communication between *Durbar* and the British government. Besides revenue powers *Diwan* exercised magisterial powers in respect of certain officers[70]. The Secretary to *Diwan* was the chief ministerial officer of the secretariat and was responsible for the efficient conduct of work. The secretariat was re-organised in 1911,1929 and in 1932. With the growth of administration and specialization it was become inevitable for the *Diwan* to diverse himself some of his powers to heads of departments.

In Cochin the formation of Legislative Council was in 1925, which consisted of 45 members of which 35 were elected. The *Diwan* was the ex-officio President. The number of members of the council was increased to 53 in 1935. A women member was nominated into the legislature[71].

In 1938 the post of minister responsible to the legislature was created and by this Cochin becomes the first state to have a ministerial government. *Diwan* continued to be in charge of departments not assigned to the ministers. After the election in 1945 two ministers were appointed. In August 1946 all departments except law and order and dewaswom were placed under the ministers[72]. The *Diwan* along with the ministers formed the cabinet of the state. The legislative council was given the power to elect a president and a deputy president in 1947. The name of the

Legislative Council was changed to Legislative Assembly in 1947. The strength of the legislature was increased to 58 and stopped the practice of nomination. All departments except law and order were placed under the ministers responsible to the legislature. The act terminated the constitutional provision of the *Diwan*. Panampilly Govinda Menon the leader of the *Praja Mandal* took charge of the Prime Minister. After the election a new ministry was formed and it continued till the integration of Travancore and Cochin in 1949[73].

A secretary to government was first appointed in 1935. A chief secretary to government was first appointed in 1946. In accordance with the recommendation of the pay revision committee, the secretariat was reorganized and the responsibility and the powers of the chief secretary were increased. On the eve of the integration of Travancore and Cochin, there were a chief secretary and five assistant secretaries[74].

The integration committee in its report recommended that the reorganized and new secretariat of the united states of Travancore and Cochin should have one chief secretary and seven secretaries on each department. In a conference of the Premier and the *Rajapramukh* held in Delhi on May 13th 1949, it was decided that the joint state should have a quantum of officers belonging to all India services such as ICS, IAS and IPS on its administration in the higher post[75].

The business of the Government was classified and distributed between the departments of the secretariat in the manner specified in the schedule of the rules of business of Travancore Cochin government. The designation of *Peishkar* and Assistant *Peishkar* were changed to Collector and Deputy Collector respectively. The designation of the revenue officer of the Taluk was continued to be Thahasildar. In 1954-55, attempts were made to reorganize the secretariat, but substantial changes in the administration were made in 1957 January 1st. In 1956 June during the presidents rule a special officer was appointed to reorganize the secretariat[76].

Malabar

After the Perumal period in the beginning of the 9th century Malabar was divided into a number of small principalities. The *Naduvazhi* or *Udayavar* was an independent ruler[77]. The village was the basic unit of administration. The village in Malabar was called *Desam*. The headman in the *Desam* was called *Desavazhi* or *Janmi*. The *Nadu* or district was ruled by the *Naduvazhi*. The *Nadu* or *Desam* constituted many *Thara* or village communities.

Every *Thara* and *Nadu* was ruled by a *Koottam* or assembly of elders. In each *Thara* certain *Tharavads* or chief houses and each *Tharavad* houses send one male representatives to the *Thara Koottam*. The several *Thara Koottam* formed a *Nattukoottam.* Another name for the members of the *Nattukoottam* was *Six hundred*[78]. The *Nadu* or districts were divided in to villages under a hereditary chief whose duty was the collection of revenue. During the Mysoorean invasion the organization of *Desams* and *Nadus* were abolished. The *Subedars* and *Faugidars* took the place of *Raja* and *Naduvazhi.* The village system was restructured. The lowest unit *Thara* was under *Parbuti* and Menon. The district was under the Thahasildar and two *Sheristadar.* The village was under *Mukhian.* The collection of revenue was the duty of the *Parbuti* of the *Thara,* the *Mukhian* gave assistance and advice to him[79].

The treaty of Srirangapattanam in 1792 provided the transfer of the whole Malabar except Wyanad. Thus the Malabar district came under the direct rule of the East India Company[80]. In 1793 the East India Company appointed its first superior and chief magistrate. Malabar was divided into six districts and sixty taluks. In 1801 for the first time collector was appointed. The frequent revolt and unrest necessitated the appointment of senior and experienced officers as collectors of the district. Collector was assisted by sub collectors or deputy collectors controlled the revenue administration of the district. There was a thahasildar in each taluks. The system of sending senior servants to Malabar continued as a tradition up to post world war period. The collector of Malabar enjoyed a status quite different from the collectors of other districts. On the eve of formation of Kerala, Malabar districts consisted of eleven taluks 1495 villages and fourteen towns. As a result of the state reorganization the whole Malabar districts were transferred to Kerala in 1956[81].

The government of Kerala had set up a committee with the chief secretary as its chairman to advice the various aspects of personnel integration. Concentration of administrative power was a feature of the administrative set up of the state at that time. So it become necessary to decentralize powers and delegates it to the heads of the departments and their district representatives as their agency primarily responsible for the execution of policies. The collectors and the revenue divisional officers became the agency to co-ordinate the administration at the district and taluk level[82].

The constitutional and administrative reforms introduced by colonial administration were not instrumental in radically changing the administrative system in these states. These reforms were deliberatively designed to accommodate or incorporate the emerging educated landlords and middle class in the society. The English administration on the one side resulted in the economic exploitation of the state. On the other hand it unleashed the forces of production from the feudal lords. It also helped in introduction of western administrative system, English education and new value system based on democracy[83].

The social and communal organsations like SNDP, NSS and Yogakshema Sabha and other similar organizations of the Muslims and Christians competed themselves to curve out their own sphere of influence in constitutional bodies of government and administration to influence the government eg. Malayalee Memorial and Ezhava Memorial submitted to the Maharaja and the Abstention Movement started in 1932 by the Ezhava, Muslims and Christians.

The British government introduced many changes in the administrative system and its agriculture and commercial policies such as abolition of slavery in 1855, starting of Public Works in 1860, opening of postal services and introduction of telegraphs, joining British Indian system of free trade adopting British Indian tariffs and the *Pandarapattom* proclamation conferring full ownership right to the tenants[84]. These polices helped to liberate both land and labourers from the feudal lords. The cultivation of cash crops, plantation and agro based industries like coir were started. New vistas of transportation and banking system were opened. New directions to the labour class and these occupations were become more profitable than the previous bonded labour and helped the emergence of a powerful middle class. Due to the effect of British administration and the effect of Christian missionaries a number of educational institutions were started. Gradually educational qualifications came to be linked with the appointment of government jobs[85].

After independence, development in the political system was the institution of democratically elected legislative assembly. Political chief executive responsible to the legislature became the administrators. In the period from 1947 –57 was spectacular at the same time frustrating too due to inter party struggle, political pressure groups, communal power and factionalism leading to ministerial instability. The decade was also eventful with multifaceted development in the administrative field. Appointment of all India personnel in the higher posts, introduction of planning and community development programme, adoption of socialist pattern of society as the national objective, state reorganisation and formation of Kerala, communist party came to power through democratic means, liberation struggle of major communal groups and the exit of the first communist ministry were the major events. At the same time political, economic and administrative developments were very much influenced by conservative law and order bureaucracy who inherited from the colonial period had their impact in the administration. In the past, administration was controlled by the king with the support of the elite class of the society. After the introduction of parliamentary democracy this power was transferred to the political elite and the bureaucrats.

From 1960 onwards political parties in Kerala are united under UDF with the leadership of Indian National Congress and the LDF under the leadership of Communist party. The possibility of changing sides and entry to alliance that came to power has really enhanced the bargaining capacity of some of the political parties more specifically the regional and communal parties like Muslim League and Kerala Congress. Kerala Congress with four groups and Muslim League have been the major beneficiaries of the administration. The course of every election the final out come will be influenced by the nature and character of the respective alliance. Alliances and counter alliances of these regional and communal parties and groups to a certain extent lead to the ministerial instability in Kerala from 1957 to 1987. The socio economic development of the state is considerably hampered because of this. Naturally the top and middle level bureaucracy in the secretariat came to play a significant role in this situation. The inexperienced political chief with no strong organized party system behind them lead to depend on bureaucracy heavily. It was criticized that there exist a wide gap between policy formulation and implementation. The practice of procedure through proper channel and red-tapism lead to delay and it was characterized the bureaucracy as a serious check in the progressive and reconstructive socio economic measures of the government. Many ministers have expressed their dissatisfaction with the bureaucratic behaviour and at the same time bureaucrats complained that the political interference affect adversely the progress of the state. The inter party and the intra party power struggle lead to intra bureaucratic and inter departmental conflict and jealousies stepped in the swam of power politics and self aggrandizement. Politicians and administrators forgot the people. Now there is an allegation that the growth of civil service is one of the reasons for acute financial crisis in the state. So it is essential to find out how the civil service reaches into the present size and who is responsible and who is the beneficiary of this.

Since 1970 civil service in Kerala started growing tremendously (figure II.1). The achievements Kerala made in different fields are closely correlated with the growth of civil services[86]. However the increase in administrative system in the higher administrative post were not based on the increase in demand. On the contrary it was due to the pressure from political as well as higher bureaucrats. None of the dominant employees organizations in Kerala has agitated against the increase in the size of civil service as the demand for increase in salary or other demands.

If examined the details of posts created since 1970 (figure. II.1), it is quite clear that there was a sudden hike in the number of higher posts. The total number of IAS officers was increased from 44 in 1969 to 178 in 2001. In 1969 the number of gazetted officers were 8529. In 2001 it was raised to 50115, i.e. Six times. The total number of employees including the teachers was 285485 and during 2002 it is 526428[87].

Fig. II.1. Increase in Number of Higher Officers in the Secretariat from 1969 to 2000

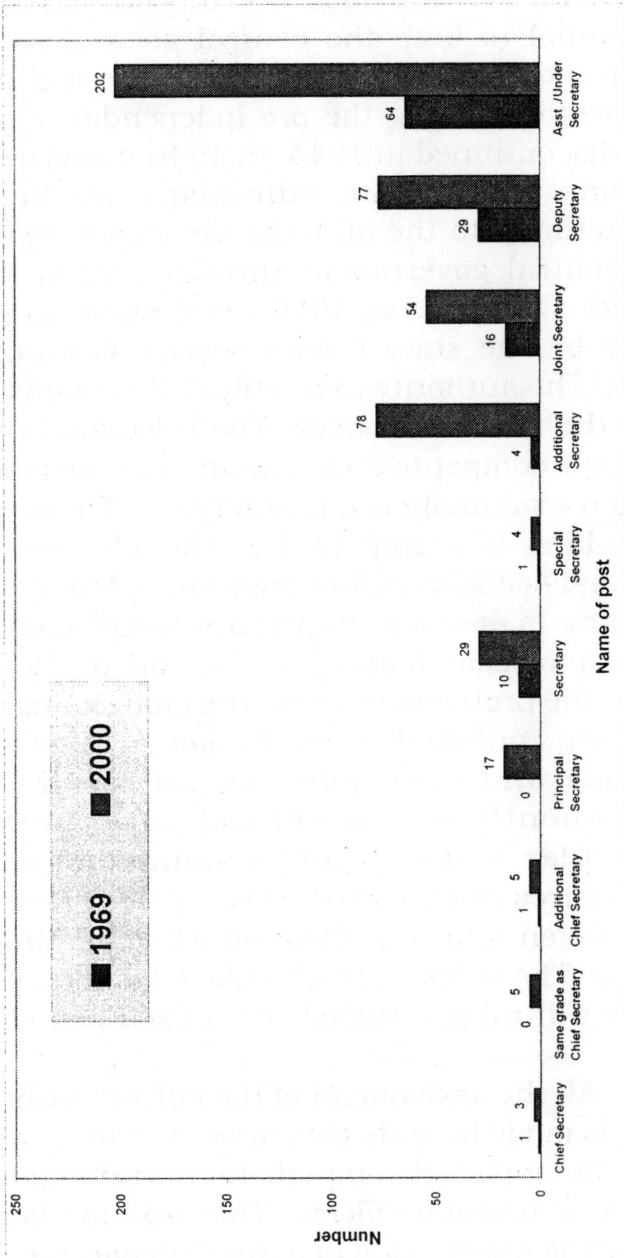

Source: Jose prakash C. R., *op.cit.*,

The IAS provides the top administrative personnel to both the central as well as state governments. The recruitment to the former Indian civil service during the pre independence period was discontinued in 1943. In 1946 it was decided to constitute Indian Administrative Service. Recruitment to the all India services is made by the central government through Union Public Service Commission (UPSC) and state service is made by the state Public Service Commission (PSC). The authority to recruit civil servants rests with the chief executives. The selection is made through competitive examinations consisting of written examination and interview. The selected candidates were imparted on the job training at National Academy of Administration, Mussori. The Training is designed to prepare the probationers for a final examination at the end of the year. When the probationers pass the final examination they are conferred in the Indian Administrative Service and each new recruit is allocated permanently by the central government to particular state cadre[88]. Candidates' merits, preferences and the existing vacancies in the state were taken into consideration while allotting the states. The officers are also placed on deputation to the central government for a fixed period.

All the assignment of the officers within the state is made by state government .A fresh recruit is firstly imparted comprehensive training in the duties of revenue officer. This training is given under the supervision of a district collector. Then they are assigned to a junior post usually in a post of sub divisional officer, deputy collector or under secretary at the state secretariat. His promotion is made according to the seniority and merit. The merit is judged on the following grounds: general knowledge of revenue affairs, promptness in replaying references from his superior and subordinates, readiness to report matters coming before him by petition, fitness with public and his ability, honesty and impartial conduct, the statement of his revenue balances and supervision over accounts, his interest in developmental work and municipal affairs and the extent of his out door work and touring. Normally an IAS officer is promoted or transferred once in three years.

Recruitment by Promotion

Selection committee in each state makes the selection of personnel by promotion to the IAS from state public service also. The chairman of the committee in every case is the chairman of the UPSC. It consisted of the following members (a) Chairman of the UPSC, (b) Chief secretary of the state, (c) Two to four members of the senior bureaucrats not below the rank of Secretary to Government and (d) A representative of the central government not below the rank of Joint Secretary[89].

In Kerala there is no separate state administrative service. The state has provincial civil service called Kerala Civil Service. The only categories of officers included in it are the deputy collectors of the revenue department. This is treated as a provincial civil service of Kerala[90]. The promotion to the IAS from the members of this service is made when they complete eight to nine years of service. A second category of conferring IAS is to those who belong to the ministerial cadre in different departments.

Administrative Reforms Committee

Administrative reforms may be defined as the "directed change of main features of an administrative system" or "improving performance by identifying the attributes and rate of bureaucratic adaptability"[91]. In order to make modifications in the administrative setup to achieve development oriented administrative efficiency, the government has constituted three committees after the formation of Kerala in 1956. The first committee was constituted under the chairmanship of late E.M.S. Namboothiripad in 1957[92]. By that time Kerala was faced with many practical problems in administration as the region of Travancore, Cochin and Malabar had different institutional setup, laws, rules and procedures as well as extend of development. The committee suggested the Ministers to be responsible for the framing of policies seeking the advice of senior civil servants. However, it wanted the Minister to leave policy implementation to the Secretary with out unnecessary restrictions. It also insists that a civil servant should be frank and fearless in giving his views and after decision making the policy should be implemented it faithfully whether his advice is accepted or rejected. It also wanted the civil servants to be politically neutral.

The second Administrative Reforms Committee was constituted in 1965 under the Chairmanship of M.K.Vellodi. The committee strongly recommended to establish a Provincial Civil Service titled "Kerala Administrative Service (KAS)" which can act as a feeder line for the All India Services, which will help to tone up administration[93]. It made recommendations for the orderly introduction of Panchayati Raj system, to notify district collector as the director of Panchayats and nominated as Chairman of Zilla Parishad. The collector should be the chief development officer and co-coordinator in the district and all district officers should submit progress reports to him. The committee also suggested stringent means to curb corruption and to monitor expenditure. It underlined clear cut definitions of responsibility through job charts for all categories of officers for improving administrative efficiency[94].

The third Administrative Reforms Committee, which came in to existence in May, 1997 under the chairmanship of Mr. E.K. Nayanar. The issue of personnel reform constitutes a major agenda of the third committee. The third Administrative Reform Committee also stressed the need for a State Civil Service[95]. The proposed Sate Administrative Service should function as the feeder line service for manning the vital administrative posts in the government. Selection to such services should be made from persons who have reached the second level of the gazetted rank in all the government departments. They should qualify a specially conducted tough competitive test with focus on knowledge of administrative and practical experience[96].

Although, the above three committees suggested many reforms for an efficient administration, the government has not taken much efforts for the effective implementation.

References

1. *Census of India 2001*, Kerala Part II, Government of India, 2001, Manager, Government of India Press, 2001, p.18.
2. *Ibid.*
3. Georges Kristoffel Lieten, *The First Communist Ministry of Kerala 1957-58*, New Delhi: K.P.Bagh and Co. 1982, p. 32.
4. V.K. Ramachandran, "Kerala's Development Achievements and Their Replicability" in Govindan Parayil (ed.) *Kerala: The Development Experience- Reflections on Sustainability and Replicability*, London: ZED Books, 2000, p.107.
5. Jean Dreze and Amartya Sen, *India's Development*, New Delhi: Oxford University Press, 1999, p. 20.
6. *Ibid.*
7. State Planning Board, *Economic Review 2000*, Thiruvananthapuram: Government of Kerala, 2000, p. 2.
8. Robin Jeffrey, *Politics, Women and Well-being, How Kerala Becomes a Model*, London: Mac Millan, 2000, p. 183.
   For more details see N.K. Bhaskaran,
   Democratic Movement in Travancore (Unpublished Ph.D Thesis), Thiruvananthapuram: Department of Political Science, University of Kerala, 1983.

9. V.K. Ramachandarn, *op. cit.,*p.107.
10. V. Balakrishnan Nair, *Social Development and Demographic Changes in South India*, New Delhi: MD Publishing Pvt. Ltd, 1994, p.25.
11. *Economic Review 2000, op. cit.,* pp. 10 & 149.
12. *Ibid.*
13. *Economc Review 2000,op. cit.,*p.150
14. *Ibid.*
15. *Ibid,*
16. V.K. Ramachandran, *op. cit.,* p.25.
17. K.P. Kannan, "Poverty Alleviation as Advancing Basic Human Capabilities: Kerala's Achievements Compared" in Govindan Parayil (ed.) *op. cit.,* p. 63.
18. V. Balakrishnan Nair, *op. cit.,*p. 33.
19. K.P.Kannan, *op. cit.,* p. 63.
20. *Economic Review 2000, op. cit.,* p. 32.
21. Joseph Tharamangalam, "The Social Roots of Kerala's Development Debacle" in M.A. Oommen (ed.) *Rethinking Development- Kerala's Development Experience Vol. II*, New Delhi: Concept Publishing Company, 1999, p.179.
22. *Ibid.*
23. *Economic Review 2000, op. cit.,* p. 2.
24. *Ibid.*
25. Joseph Tharamangalam, *op. cit.,* p.185.
26. *Ibid.*
27. Mridul Eapen, *Rural Industrialization in Kerala: Its Dynamism and Local Linkage*, New Delhi: Manmohar Publications, 2001, p.40.
28. B.A. Prakash (ed*) Keralas Economic Development- Issues and Problems*, New Delhi: Sage Publications, 1994, p.40.
29. M.A. Oommen, "Kerala and New World Order-Some Tentative Hypothesis", *Mainstream,*November 26, 1994, p.101.
30. K.P. Kannan, *op. cit.,* p. 58.
31. S.N. Sadasivan, *Administration and Social Development in Kerala*, Thiruvananthapuram: Indian Institute of Public Administration Regional Branch, 1988, p. 5.
32. *Ibid.*
33. Richard W. Franke and Barbara H. Chasin, *Kerala- Development Through Radical Reforms*, New Delhi: Promilla & Co. Publishers, 1992, p. 6.
34. S.N. Sadasivan, *op. cit.,* p. 5.
35. E.M.S. Namboothiripad, *Kerala Charithram Marxist Veekhshanathil (M)*, Thiruvananthapuram: Chintha Publications, 1997, p. 36.
36. V.K. Ramachandran, *op. cit.,* p.100.

37. T.J. Nossitter, *Communism in Kerala- A Study of Political Adaptation*, New Delhi: Oxford University Press, 1982, p.71.
38. K.P. Kannan, *op. cit.*, p.58.
39. A. Sreedhara Menon, *Kerala and Freedom Struggle*, Kottayam: DC Books, 1997, p. 60.
40. K.P. Kannan, *op. cit.*, p.59.
41. T.J. Nossitter, *op. cit.*, p.71.
42. K.P. Kannan, *op. cit.*, p.59.
43. A. Sreedhara Menon, *A Survey of Kerala History*, Madras: S. Viswanathan Printers and Publishers, 1994, p. 331.
44. *Ibid.*
45. P. Radhakrishnan, *Peasant Struggles, Land Reforms and Social Change in Malabar 1836-1982*, New Delhi: Sage Publication, 1989, p.111.
46. *Ibid,* p.112.
47. Richard W. Franke and Barbara H. Chasin, *op. cit.*, p.52.
48. P. Radhakrishnan, *op. cit.*, p. 272.
49. V. Balakrishnan Nair, *op. cit.*, p. 52.
50. Elamkulam P. N. Kunjan Pillai, *Studies in Kerala History*, Kottayam: National Books Stall, 1970, p.41.
51. Government of Kerala, *Kerala State Gazetteer*, Thiruvananthapuram: Government Press, 1986, p.10.
52. A. Sreedhara Menon, *op. cit.*, p. 31.
53. *Ibid.*
54. Kerala State Gazetteer, *op. cit.*, p. 11.
55. K. Sukumaran Nair, *op. cit.*, p.3.
56. K. Saradamani, *Matriliny Transferred*, New Delhi: Sage Publications, 1999, p. 42.
57. A. Sreedhara Menon, *Kerala and Freedom Struggle*, *op. cit.*, p. 20.
58. Kerala State Gazetteer, *op. cit.*, p.16.
59. S.N. Sadasivan, *op. cit.*, p.34.
60. Kerala State Gazetteer, *op. cit.*,p.19.
61. *Ibid.*
62. S.N. Sadasivan, *op. cit.*, p. 34.
63. A. Balakrishnan Nair, *The Government and Politics of Kerala*, Thiruvananthapuram: Indira Publication, 1994, p.14.
64. K. Sukumaran Nair, *op. cit.*,p.VI.
65. *Ibid.*
66. A Balakrishnan Nair. Land Marks in the *Admistration of Kerala*, Thiruvananthapuram: Indian Institute of Public Administration, 1997, p. 21.

67. A. Sreedhara Menon, *op. cit.*, p. 47.
68. Kerala State Gazetteer, *op. cit.*, p. 27.
69. C. Achutha Menon, *Cochin State Manuel*, Eranakulam: 1941, pp. 118-119
70. K. Sukumaran Nair, *op. cit.*, p.6.
71. A. Sreedhara Menon, *A Survey of Kerala History*, *op. cit.*, p.289.
72. *Ibid.*
73. K. Sukumaran Nair, *op. cit.*, p.14.
74. A. Balakrishnan Nair, *op. cit.*, p.24.
75. S. N. Sadasivan, *op. cit.*, p.34.
76. *Ibid.*
77. Kerala State Gazetteer, *op. cit.*,p. 20.
78. *Ibid.*
79. *Ibid.*
80. A. Sreedhara Menon, *Kerala and Freedom Struggle*, *op. cit.*, p.20.
81. Government of Kerala, *Administrative Reforms Commission Report*, Vol.-I. Thiruvananthapuram: (Chairman E.M.S. Namboothiripad) Government Press, 1958, p.13.
82. *Ibid.*
83. J. Prabhash, *Affirmative Action and Social Change- Social Mobility of the Dalits*, New Delhi: Anmol Publishers Pvt., Ltd. 2001, p. 31.
84. *Ibid.*
85. *Ibid.*
86. Jose Prakash C.R, "Civil Service Yengane Valuthai" (M), Thiruvananthapuram: *Bharana Chakkram*, August 2001, pp. 12-13.
87. *Ibid.* See also
    (1) *Gradation List (as on 1-7-2001), Indian Administrative Service-Kerala Cadre*, Thiruvananthapuram: 2001.
    (2) Government of Kerala,
    Seniority List of Additional Secretaries, Joint Secretaries, Deputy Secretaries to Government in the Administrative Secretariat as on 1-1-2000, Thiruvananthapuram: Government Press, 2000.
88. B.R. Verma, *op. cit.*, p.140.
89. *Ibid.*
90. R.K. Suresh Kumar, *op. cit.*, p. 251.
91. P. R. Dubashi, *Administrative Reforms in Perspectives*, Thiruvananthapuram: Indian Institute of Public Administration (Regional Branch), 1985, p.11
92. Government of Kerala, *Report of Administrative Reforms Committee*, Vol. I & II, Chairman E.M.S. Namboothiripad, *op. cit.*,

93. Government of Kerala, *Report of Administrative Reorganization and Economy Committee*, Chairman M.K. Vellodi, Thiruvananthapuram: Government Press, 1967, Part I, pp.70-71.
94. *Ibid.* p. 71.
95. Government of Kerala, *Report of Administrative Reforms Committee*(Interim), Chairman E.K. Nayanar, Thiruvananthapuram: Government Press, 2000, Part I, p. 4.
96. *Kerala Kaumudi*, August 18, 2002.

3

Socio-Economic Background of Higher Bureaucracy

The socio-economic background of higher bureaucracy and its attitude, values and role perception are very closely inter-related. The formulation and implementation of various programmes tend to reflect the attitudes and perception of the civil servants, which are not only a corollary of their socio-economic background but also the ideas and values that they have acquired as a result of their exposure to the world outside. Besides, the civil servants after entering the steel frame have acquired new attitudes and values that are characteristics of the bureaucracy. The elitist character of the bureaucracy, a dominant feature of the colonial administration, continues to remain unchanged. However, it is a fact that the new recruitment policy including reservation for socially and educationally deprived sections of the society in the post-independent India has to a small extent broadened the socio-economic base of the higher bureaucracy. But it should be pointed out that a slight advancement of the social base of bureaucracy has not significantly altered its elitist character. The civil servants recruited from SC/ST and other backward classes have more or less adapted the attitudes and values of the higher bureaucracy. With this in mind, an attempt has been made to study the socio-economic and educational background of the higher bureaucracy in Kerala to determine at what extend their attitudes and values are conditioned by their background.

The officers of the Indian Administrative Service hold the key executive posts all over the country. So there should be an ideal representation in its memberships drawn from various occupational, geographical and social groups. This is expected to ensure such social composition of bureaucracy, which would be self-regulating and responsive. The concept of representative bureaucracy advocates that the socio – economic composition of bureaucracy should resemble the society as a whole with every social group have its own spokesman in the bureaucracy to guard its interests.

In India relevance of representative bureaucracy become a matter of supreme importance in the context of development administration. India has been involved in a gigantic programme of development. After independence a large number of programmes, schemes and projects for socio-economic development involving huge investments were launched under successive five year plans. The role of higher bureaucracy in the country has also undergone profound change with the change in functions of government. The effectiveness with which they perform their roles to accomplish the goals of administration is determined to a large extend by their skills, knowledge, behaviour, attitudes and values.

Assuming that certain attitudes of mind tends to be associated with the particular type of social origin, it may be argued that something in general gained the pattern of society and the characteristics of various sections constituting it get more wholesome reflection in the behaviour and action of the members of higher bureaucracy.

A series of studies have been made with regard to the socio-economic background of higher bureaucracy in India to understand how representative the country's bureaucracy is. Any general conclusion drawn from the study of their social, educational, economic and cultural background should be of interest to students of public administration from the standpoint of an understanding of the persons who help in policy formulation and execution.

The behaviour of an individual in any organization is greatly influenced by the existing norms and values and there is continuous interaction between organization and individuals. According to V. Subramaniam "The bureaucrats carry their class attitudes and prejudices into the official life and only when all classes or castes are properly represented in the bureaucracy, their different needs and interest find due attention"[1]. Some scholars believe that the social origin of bureaucrats have little reference to their pattern of behaviour. For them what is more relevant is the prevailing administrative culture descending from one generation to another. It is difficult to draw any hard and fast conclusion in this regard.

The relationship between the background and behaviour is largely related. Individuals carrying his specific traits into administration cannot be disputed. His socio-economic background shapes these traits. So it will be interesting to find out their socio–economic background such as, the economic class to which they belong, personal attributes they displays, educational status and sources of income of the family etc. and analyse at what extent his personality and other innate traits reflect on policy outcomes. Further, an investigation of the social background of the higher bureaucracy would also facilitate a comparative study of the conditions in other states of the country. This will also help in working out comparable trends. The perusal of the studies conducted on bureaucracy reveals the fact that most of them had mainly focused on the structure and its response to various problems.

The study of the socio-economic background of the higher bureaucracy of Kerala assumes importance, as it throws up significant insights into their status, social and educational background and occupation, motivating factor to join the civil service, spouse's occupation, political preferences and their parent's attitude etc. During the last decade significant changes had occurred in the composition of the entrants to the civil service. The number of engineering and medical professionals entering the civil service is also on the rise.

It would also be useful to understand the kind of people recruited to the secretariat and at the district level because they are expected to carry out development administration. In the decentralized system of administration the higher bureaucrats in the state of Kerala are to work with the members of the local self-government for the realization of administrative goals.

The present chapter deals with the study of higher bureaucracy in Kerala and their socio-economic background. The data on the socio-economic background of the higher bureaucracy have been collected through a structured questionnaire, administered by the researcher. The names of IAS officers of the Kerala cadre was collected from the gradation list of IAS officers published by the government of Kerala[2]. A total of 200 questionnaires had been distributed, of which 178 officers were in service and the rest were retired personnel. Of the 178 officers in the gradation list, few were on leave or doing higher studies/ on deputation abroad. Out of the total 178 officers, 90 officers returned the questionnaire duly filled with their specific comments. Two officers however returned the questionnaire unfilled.

The response of the officers towards the interview schedule was a mixed one. Some of them were very enthusiastic and offered their ideas and insights. The attitude of some officers was very unhelpful. A few of them took an undemocratic and hostile attitude towards the researcher. This is clear from one of the bureaucrat's response that he had "*nothing to discuss*". Some others expressed their reservations, as they feared that any disclosure would bring in disciplinary action. A few officers were callous and showed utter disregard.

Of the 90 respondents 74 respondents are male and the rest female. Even though women are highly educated in Kerala, their number in the IAS cadre is considerably less. Even at the national level women representation in the higher bureaucracy is negligible. For instance during 1985, 311 were women and in 1992 their number was 445 out of 4500[3]. In the case of IPS it was 0.02 percent in 1992 and regarding IFS it stood at 11.28 percent[4]. Very few women could be found in politics, administration, economic fields, management and in trade union activities. In India the women representation in the Parliament is only 7.73 percent. However, in Japan one of the most economically advanced countries in the world it is only 2.3 percent. The women representation of some of the countries are given in figure III.1.

Fig. III.1. Women Representation in Legislatures of Some Countries.

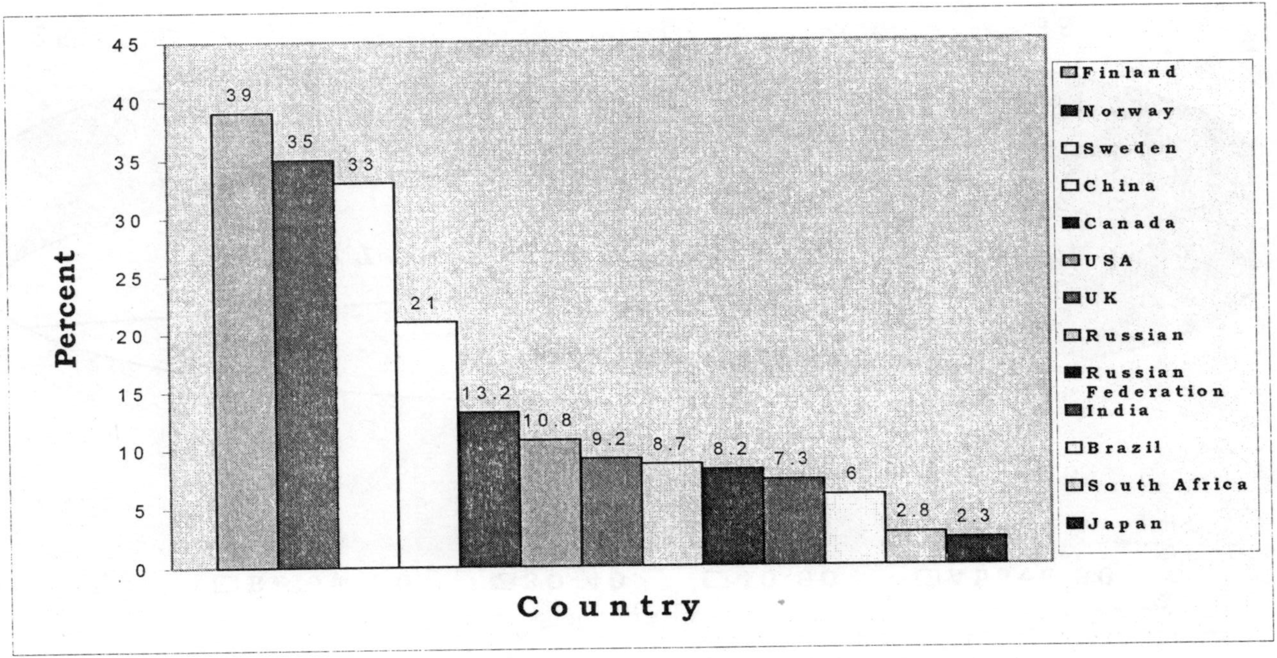

Source: VMFT News letter, Thiruvananthapuram, Vol.7, No.1,January 1995

Fig. III.2. Age Group of Higher Bureaucrats in Kerala

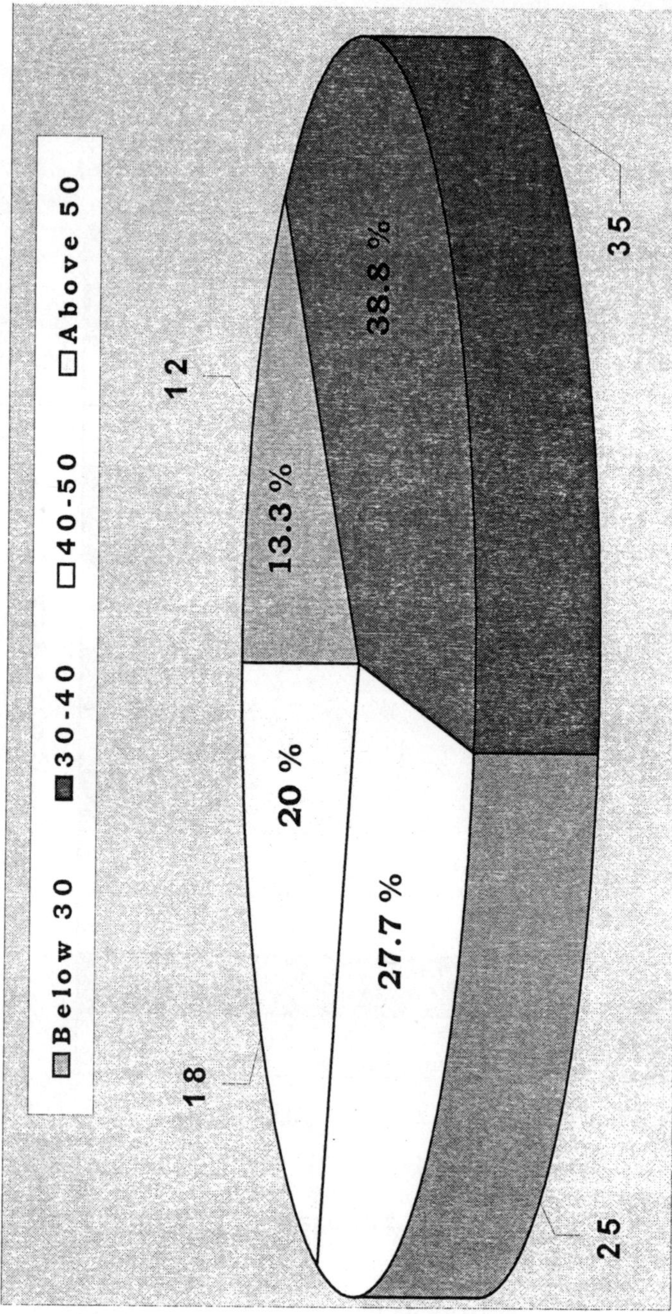

Source: Survey data

Out of the total parliamentarians, men constitute about 90 percent. In the 12th Kerala Legislature there are only 8 women members. Though a large number of NGOs and non-official activists are working in India as decision makers, women's position still remains within their family. According to Jayanth Kumar Banthya, National Census Commissioner & Registrar General, in Kerala the women working population is the lowest in the country and it is 14 percent. However, in Maharashtra, it is 40 percent[5].

The age of the higher bureaucracy is an important factor, because it tends to determine the nature, role preference and value orientation of the officers. Out of the 90 respondents 12 officers are below 30 years (13.3 percent), 35 officers are between the age group of 30 & 40 (38.8 percent), 25 officers are between the age group of 40 & 50 (27.7 percent) and 18 officers are above 50 years (20 percent). The figure III.2 shows that the middle age category dominates the higher bureaucracy.

The information regarding the home state is interesting. India is a multi religious and multi linguistic country. In order to maintain an all India balance of civil service, a certain percentage of officers from outside Kerala are found in the Kerala cadre. The orientation and value preferences of these officers may differ. The table III.1. shows that 63.3 percent of the civil servants are working in their home state. The Tamil Brahmins dominated in the Travancore civil service. The natives submitted many petitions and memorials against this. The "Malayalee Memorial" of 1891 is an expression of the resentment of the educated people of Travancore[6].

Seven officers out of ninety responded were belonging to the neighbouring Tamilnadu state. Next to Tamilnadu comes Uttar Pradesh and Bihar with five each. Four are from Rajasthan, three from Andhra Pradesh and three from West Bengal. Two officers each from Orissa and Punjab and one each from Delhi and Sikkim are also figured in the sample.

Table. III. 1. Home state of IAS officers in Kerala

Sl. No.	*Native state of officers*	*No. of officers responded*	*Percent*
1	Kerala	57	63.3
2	Tamilnad	7	7.7
3	Uttar Pradesh	5	5.5
4	Bihar	5	5.5
5	Andhra Pradesh	3	3.3
6	Orissa	2	2.2
7	Rajasthan	4	4.4
8	West Bengal	3	3.3
9	Punjab	2	2.2
10	Sikkim	1	1.1
11	Delhi	1	1.1
	Total	90	100

Source: Survey data.

In Kerala there are no great disparities between rural and urban areas. Historically there was a fair spread of educational and health facilities in rural areas, which has been kept up by public policies. With the rapid growth of commercial agriculture there existed a well developed road transport system which further strengthened in the post independence period making almost every village in Kerala more accessible[7]. The rural-urban impacts influence the behavioural pattern and attitude of the higher bureaucracy. In Kerala the rural urban difference is comparatively very less as compared to other Indian states and the difference in rural urban life style is now only in a very low degree because

Table. III. 2. The state wise urban-rural classification of IAS officers

Sl. No.	*State*	*No. of Officers respon -dents*	*Rural*	*Percent*	*Urban*	*Percent*
1.	Kerala	57	27	30	30	33.3
2.	UP	5	3	3.3	2	2.2
3.	Bihar	5	3	3.3	2	2.2
4.	Andhra Pradesh	3	2	2.2	1	1.1
5.	Rajasthan	4	2	2.2	2	2.2
6.	Sikkim	1			1	1.1
7.	West Bengal	3			3	3.3
8.	Punjab	2			2	2.2
9.	Orissa	2	1		1	1.1
10.	Delhi	1			1	1.1
11.	Tamilnad	7	2	2.2	5	5.5
	Total	90	40	44.4	50	55.5

Source: Survey data.

modern technology and communication facilities have reduced the gap. In Kerala 55.5 percent of officers belong to urban areas and 44. 4 percent of officers are having rural background. It is also interesting to note that more than 60 percent of the female officers belong to urban areas. Among the 57 officers from Kerala 47 percent of them belongs to rural areas and 53 percent of the officers are from urban areas. The State- wise rural –urban classification is given in table III.2. A survey of 289 IAS officers belonging to different states conducted in early 90s showed that 76.55 percent are from urban areas and the rest came from rural villages[8].

Better educational facilities and higher income level in the urban areas resulted in urban population being over represented in the civil service. Due to expansion of educational facilities in rural areas, the representation of the rural people in public service has also been increasing. This is true in the case of Kerala.

Mother Tongue

The language of the civil servants and the ability of the officers to communicate in different languages can reveal certain aspects related to the problem of administration.

Now English has been accepted as the common language. The poor strata of the society must understand the language of the higher bureaucrats. In the present study, 60 percent officers' mother tongue is Malayalam. Three officers' home state is Kerala but recorded their mother tongue as Tamil. Followed by Malayalam 11.1 percent officer's mother tongue is Tamil, 16.6 percent Hindi, 3.3 percent Telugu, 3.3 percent Bengali, 2.2 percent Punjabi, 2.2 percent Oria and 1.1 percent Sikkimese (table III.3). The officers are usually taught the regional language of the state, which he was allotted. In order to have the social background of the civil servants, it is

Table III . 3. The Mother Tongue of IAS Officers in Kerala

Sl. No.	*Language*	*No. of officers responded*	*Percent*
1	Malayalam	54	60
2	Hindi	15	16.6
3	Tamil	10	11.1
4	Telugu	3	3.3
5	Bengali	3	3.3
6	Punjabi	2	2.2
7	Oriya	2	2.2
8	Sikkimese	1	1.1
	Total	90	100

Source: Survey data.

necessary to include the religious back ground of the civil servants. India is a secular state and no religious discrimination is possible for any post under the Indian constitution. But it is interesting to understand the religious composition of IAS officers. Through this it is also possible to understand whether minority communities are adequately represented or not.

India is a multi-religious country where majority of the people are Hindus. The society is divided into a number of castes and sub castes. Kerala, although small in size, is a multi-religious state. Its population consists of three major religious groups namely the Hindus, Christians and Muslims. Hinduism is the widely professed religion and it is the religious faith of the majority and about 58 percent of the population during all the census periods were Hindus. Christians constitutes the second largest and the Muslims third[9]. Figure III. 3. shows that among the 90 respondents 71.1 percent officers are Hindus, 26.6 percent are Christians and 1.1 percent Buddhist. Even though Muslims are about 20 percent of the total population they are under represented. There are only 6 Muslim officers in the IAS gradation list.[10]

Fig.III.3. Religious background of IAS officers in Kerala

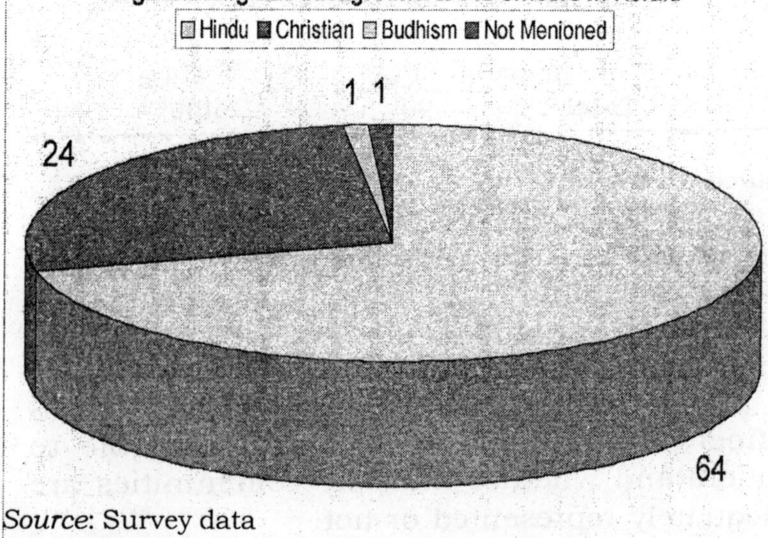

Source: Survey data

The caste-based breakup of respondents is given in table. III. 4. From the table it is clear that the respondents are largely from the forward caste. Brahmins constitute 17.7 percent, Christians (forward caste) 21.1 percent, Nairs 18.8 percent and Kshathriyas 3.3 percent. These are the major forward caste communities in Kerala. The Ezhava community represent 3.3 percent, SC 10.0 percent and ST 1.1 percent. 3 officers did not specify the caste and mentioned as 'general' and 11 officers did not respond to this question.

The analysis of caste in this type of study is important. Caste influences people in diverse ways. The higher bureaucracy is also not free from caste or its vicious effects. A number of officers are skeptical in furnishing this information. The representation of SC is 10 percent and the respondents from this category indicated that they were not able to fully utilize the facilities of reservation. The representation of the two major communities, the Ezhava and Muslim is minimal. The Ezhava community is a major constituent part of the Hindu fold and their representation in higher bureaucracy is only 3.3 percent and there is no Muslim representation in this study. The table III.4. indicates that the general share of backward communities in the service is disproportionate to their demographic strength in the society. Usually officers belonging to the SC/ST or backward community very rarely reaches in the glamorous posts like chief secretary or home secretary. Administrators have often failed to fill up vacancies reserved for SC/ST and backward classes candidates because of their deliberate caste prejudices[11]. The present study reveals that the position of SC and ST categories in Kerala is better compared to other states[12].

Table III. 4. Caste Pattern of IAS Officers in Kerala

Sl. No.	*Caste*	*No. of officers responded*	*Percent*
1	Christians	19	21.1
2	Nairs	17	18.8
3	Brahmin	16	17.7
4	SC	9	10
5	Kshathriyas	3	3.3
6	Ezhava	3	3.3
7	Buddhists*	3	3.3
8	ST	1	1.1
9	Kamma	1	1.1
10	Adi Dravida	1	1.1
11	Chakkala Nair	1	1.1
12	Kayastha	1	1.1
13	Kurmi	1	1.1
14	No response	11	12.2
15	General	3	3.3
	Total	90	100

Source: Survey data.

Educational Qualification

Education is the process of training and developing knowledge, skill, mind, character etc. especially by formal schooling. The concept of education is not merely to impart knowledge to the pupils in certain subjects but also bring him up or develop in him those habits and attitudes, which enable him to face problems head on. It is at the school stage that the formulation of the super structure of the university education is laid down[13]. An analysis of the educational background of the higher bureaucracy is all the more important as it provides an useful insight into the ability to take matters into their stride while in administration. It also gives a clue to the fact that whether the administrator is a generalist or a specialist.

Table III. 5. shows that, of the 90 respondents 74.4 percent are postgraduate degree holders, 4.4 percent are graduates, 5.5 percent doctors, 11.1 percent engineering and 4.4 percent other degree holders including LLB. 17.7 percent officers are having additional degrees like Ph.D, M.Phil, MBA, LLB etc. Majority of the postgraduates holds their degree in social sciences. Among the 67 postgraduate degree holders, 10 are having post graduation in economics. The officers having masters degree are increasing. Another trend is that the number of candidates with professional degrees in engineering and medicine get selected to IAS are increasing. Table III. 6. shows that, in a national level study of IAS probationers of the 1992 batch, the largest number (56.25 percent) of the probationers are engineers followed by arts graduates (17.8 percent), natural science (10 percent), medicine (7.5 percent) and commerce (5 percent). There is one probationer each from veterinary science and law.[14]

Table III. 5. Educational qualification of IAS officers of Kerala

Sl. No.	*Degree secured*	*No. of officers responded*	*Percent*
1	BA, B.Sc, B.Com	4	4.4
2	MA, M.Sc, M.Com	67	74.4
3	Engineering	10	11.1
4	Doctors	5	5.5
5	Other degrees	4	4.4
	Total	90	100

Source: Survey data

Table III. 6. Educational qualification of IAS officers at the national level

Sl.No.	*Degree obtained*	*Percent*
1	Engineering	56.25
2	Arts	17.8
3	Science graduates	10
4	Medicine	7.5
5	Commerce	5
6	Post graduation	47.5

Source: Rajendrakumar & Kalpana Bhatnagar.

Many officers have obtained their additional qualification like MBA, Ph.D, LLB etc. after successfully passing the civil service examination. A study conducted in West Bengal in 1989 shows that, 26 out of 46 officers had masters degree and 19 officers possessed bachelors degree[15]. A study conducted in Haryana revealed that out of 16 officers 14 are post graduates and 2 graduates[16]. In Himachal Pradesh, out of 16 IAS officers 15 are postgraduate degree holders and one bachelor degree holder. An analysis of 444 IAS officers of UP cadre in respect of whom information about their educational background is readily available, as many as 26 had doctorates, 326 had post graduate qualifications in one or more subjects and 92 were degree holders in one or more subjects like engineering, law, management, mathematics or humanities[17]. A survey of 289 officers from different state cadres of the country conducted in early 1990s showed that 13.49 percent were graduates, 82.7 percent post graduates and 3.81 percent have doctorate degree[18].

Medium of Instruction

The students educated in English medium school or public school background have better chance for getting in to the service. The number of officers who went to the English medium or public school was proportionately much higher than those who went to government schools with regional language as the medium of instruction. The study reveals that the medium of instruction of 56.6 percent officers at school level was English and for 43.3 percent officers at school level was regional language (table. III.7). At the college level 98.8 percent officers had their medium of instruction as English. One officer belongs to Andhra Pradesh whose medium of instruction was

Table III.7. Medium of instruction of IAS officers from Kerala at school level

Sl. No.	*Language*	*No. of. officers responded*	*Percent*
1	English	51	56.6
2	Regional language	39	43.3
	Total	**90**	**100**

Source: Survey data.

Table III. 8. Medium of instruction of IAS officers from Kerala at college level

Sl. No.	*Language*	*No. of. officers responded*	*Percent*
1	English	89	98.8
2	Regional language	1	1.1
	Total	90	100

Source : Survey data.

regional language (table III. 8). In a study on the background and attitude of IAS probationers of 1992 batch, the medium of instruction for 47.7 percent of respondents at school level and higher secondary level were English and the rest in regional languages[19]. Similarly a study conducted in West Bengal reveals the same trend[20]. For instance 54.35 percent of officers' medium of instruction at school level was English and the percentage of regional language schooling was 43 percent[21].

The study clearly establishes the fact that the majority of the IAS officers had English medium education throughout especially in the best schools and colleges. Many of the children belonging to the weaker sections and other working classes could not afford education in some of the English medium private schools mainly because of the cost of education in such schools. Moreover, it is important to note that there exist a basic difference in the course content and the quality of teaching in English medium private schools and government schools. The study shows that the elite schools have an edge over ordinary schools and therefore the products from these English medium schools have a better chance of getting into the central services. Thus it can be established that majority of the recruits into IAS hails from upper and middle class backgrounds. Thus, the character of the civil service in terms of their socio-economic background continues to be elitist in nature, although a small section belongs to the lower classes get into the service due to the reservation and hard work.

Contribution from Different Universities

Most of the studies on the educational background of the IAS recruits of various states clearly shows that majority have postgraduate and professional degrees. The present study also reveals the same trend. As the table. III.9. reveals 42.2 percent are from Kerala University and 13.3 percent from Madras University. 8.8 percent from Delhi University followed by 3.3 percent each from Cochin University and Punjab University, 2.2 percent each from Calcutta University, Central Universities and Andhra University, 6.6 percent from different IITs, 1 each from Rajasthan University, Patna University, Annamalai University, Baroda University, Bangalore University, Agricultural University, Calicut University and Regional Engineering College, Mangalore. 5.5 percent officers did not mentioned about their University. Next to Kerala University, Madras University produced maximum number of officers in this study. 95.6 percent of the higher civil servants have postgraduate and professional degrees and most of them have attended the best State and Central Universities as well as IITs and RECs.As the table III.9 shows, 42.2 percent officers belong to the Kerala cadre have their degrees taken from Kerala University followed by Madras University. The main reason for this is that Madras posses a tradition in getting into the civil service which other cities like Bombay and Culcutta lacks.[22] The higher education obtained from these universities could provide the recruits a better comprehension of the socio-economic reality and therefore they are well equipped to face the challenges.

Table III. 9. Representation of Different Universities in the IAS Cadre

Sl. No.	*Name of the university*	*No. of officers responded*	*Percent*
1	Kerala University	38	42.2
2	Madras University	12	13.3
3	Delhi University	8	8.8
4	IITs	6	6.6
5	Cochin University	3	3.3
6	Punjab University	3	3.3
7	Andhra University	2	2.2
8	Calcutta University	2	2.2
9	Central Universities	2	2.2
10	Calicut University	1	1.1
11	Rajasthan University	1	1.1
12	Patna University	1	1.1
13	Annamalai University	1	1.1
14	Lucknow University	1	1.1
15	MS University of Baroda	1	1.1
16	Bangalore University	1	1.1
17	Kerala Agricultural University	1	1.1
18	REC Mangalore	1	1.1
19	Not mentioned	5	5.5
	Total	90	100

Source: Survey data.

Education of Parents

Educational background of the parents plays a crucial role in the motivation and interest in the development of their career. For instance, majority of the recruit's parents had good educational backgrounds. As table III.10. shows

35.5 percent have bachelors degree, 16.6 percent are post graduates, 18.8 percents of respondent's fathers are with professional degree, 21.1 percent are matriculate, 3.3 percent are having other technical qualifications. Only 3.3 percent officer's parents have no formal degree.

Table III. 10. Education of IAS officers' parents in Kerala

Sl. No.	*Education of parents of IAS officers*	*No. of officers responded*	*Percent*
1	Matriculation	19	21.1
2	Degree	32	35.5
3	Post graduation	15	16.6
4	Professionals	17	18.8
5	Any other degree	3	3.3
6	Below matriculation	3	3.3
7	No response	1	1.1
	Total	90	100

Source: Survey data.

The education achieved by the parents have a direct correlation to the position attained by their children, this has been proved in this study. The table III.10 reveals that more than 70 percent officers' parents are highly educated. Most of the officers have mentioned their fathers' educational qualification. But some officers have mentioned their mothers' educational qualification as well. More than 50 percent officers' mothers are graduates or post graduates.

Occupation of Parents

Occupation has been widely accepted as one of the criteria of social status. The study of the occupation of parents provides an insight into the family background of the civil servants. This is because the socio-economic background and attitude and perception of the officers are closely related. Moreover, it would enable us to understand the social composition of the

Table III.11. Occupational background of IAS officers' parents in Kerala

Sl. No.	*Parents' occupation*	*No. of officers responded*	*Percent*
1	Teacher	15	16.6
2	Doctor	3	3.3
3	Engineer	7	7.7
4	Business	2	2.2
5	Executive	17	18.8
6	Govt: service	32	35.5
7	Lawyers	3	3.3
8	Agriculture	2	2.2
9	Any other	6	6.6
10	No response	3	3.3
	Total	90	100

Source: Survey data.

bureaucracy that is to what extend different social groups are represented in the bureaucracy. In other words, the representative character of the bureaucracy can be understood by studying the occupation of the parents. This becomes important in the context of growing inequality in the present day context of globalisation where admission to professional courses is determined by money and power.[23]

Table III.11 reveals that majority of the officers' parents are government servants. About 17 percent of them are teachers, 35.5 per cent are government servants, 18.8 percent are executives, 3.3 percent doctors, 7.7 engineers, 3.3 percent lawyers, 2.2 percent agriculturists and the rest belongs to the miscellaneous class. 3.3 percent of the respondents did not answer this specific question. More than 50 percent officers' mothers are employed and most of them are teachers.

The educational and occupational attainment of parents determines the career goal of their children. The educated and well-employed parents are anxious about their children's education and career. Education below matriculation and agricultural profession are negligible (3.3 and 2.2 respectively). About 3.3 per cent officers refused to reveal information about their parents' occupation. This might be due to growing alienation and discrimination among respondents in identifying themselves with their fathers' lower level occupation.

A similar trend has been noticed in the study on higher bureaucracy in other states as well. In a study of the background and attitudes of IAS probationers of 1992 batch, 56.25 percent probationers responded that their parents were in government service.[24] Next comes agriculture 12.5 percent and teaching 10 percent. A study of 289 officers of several states conducted in early 1990s showed that 67.63 percent officers parents came from service sector, 11.15 from business, and 21.22 per cent from farming[25]. Similar trend has been noticed in the studies on higher bureaucracy in West Bengal[26], Haryana and Himachal Pradesh[27].

Compared with other states, the number of IAS entrants with an agricultural background of parents is less in Kerala. Probably this may be due to the fact that in Kerala most of the farmer community belongs to middle level peasantry with some surplus. On the contrary, the situation is different in the north Indian states were the parents belong to the very rich land owning class.

The study once again proves that children of the parents in government service including executives and professionally qualified dominate Kerala higher bureaucracy. About 80 percent of officers' parents are employed at higher levels. From this we can say that the better-off section of the society, had better opportunity for proper education and this helped them to reach this coveted career.

Source of Income of Family

Source of income of family confirm the parent's occupation. Table III.12 shows that 72.2

percent of the respondents stated that the government service is their source of income. 15.5 percent mentioned that land is their major source of income. Another 6.6 percent officers mentioned that house, vehicles and business are additional source of income. Similarly, 5.5 percent of the respondents have additional income from other sources like shares. About 27.7 percent officers honestly revealed their additional sources of income. Even the officers whose main sources of income is salary have stated that their parents and spouses have own land. Most of the officers have houses in urban areas, which are rented out to earn additional income.

Table III.12. Source of Income of the IAS Officers' Family in Kerala

Sl. No.	*Source of income*	*No. of officers responded*	*Percent*
1	Service	65	72.2
2	Land	14	15.5
3	House	2	2.2
4	Vehicle	2	2.2
5	Business	2	2.2
6	Any other	5	5.5
	Total	90	100

Source: Survey data.

In this connection it is useful to refer a national level study conducted among 289 officers in the 1990s. The study reveals that 90 percent of them belongs to the higher and middle income groups and only 7 percent belongs to the low-income group[28]. This study also shows that most of the recruits (75.55 percent) came from urban areas. Similar trend has been noticed in the states like West Bengal[29], Haryana and Himachal Pradesh[30]. Thus it is clear that like in other states, in Kerala also the urban, upper caste and upper middle class dominate the higher echelons of administration. These officers are the recently urbanized and educated strata of the rich peasantry in the countryside. Thus there is continuity in the socio-economic background of the higher bureaucracy and the elite character of the bureaucracy remains unchanged.

Occupational Experience Before Joining IAS

Table III.13 shows that 30 percent of the officers had been teaching before entering into IAS. Researchers constituted 7.7 percent, executives 13.3 percent, fresher from college 27.7 percent and coming from other jobs 21.1 percent. About 72.2 percent of the officers had worked in different capacities before joining in the administrative service. But the situation is slightly different at the national level. This is clear from a national level study on IAS probationers of the 1992 batch, which shows that most of the recruits are fresh from college and have little previous work experience[31].

Table III. 13. Occupational experience of officers before joining IAS

Sl. No.	*Response of IAS officers*	*No. of officers responded*	*Percent*
1	Teaching	27	30
2	Research	7	7.7
3	Executive	12	13.3
4	Fresh from college	25	27.7
5	Other job	19	21.1
	Total	90	100

Source: Survey data.

Marital status

Four out of 90 officers responded were unmarried and 86 were married, among these 2 were widowers and one divorcee. Marriage between civil servants after joining the service is a common incidence. This is clear from the table III. 14. It was considered as an indicative of their attitude towards their own life. The elitist nature of the service compels them to remain in the same group. Thus the solidarity and unity of the elitist service is maintained. There is hardly any attempt to break this elitist character. It is a fact that officers after joining the service look for a marriage from a very high family. Besides, the rich and influential people try to net them to have family relationship. The study clearly established the fact that majority of the officers have marital alliance with rich classes. Majority of the respondents, spouses are housewifes with out any formal occupation. Another important aspect of the family is that majority of the respondents' children prefer executive, medical, engineering or IAS profession.

Table III. 14. Occupation of IAS officers spouses

Sl. No.	*Spouses occupation*	*No. of officers responded*	*Percent*
1	IAS	11	12.2
2	Doctors	-	-
3	Engineer	5	5.5
4	Teaching	1	1.1
5	Executives	3	3.3
6	House wife	52	57.7
7	IPS	2	2.2
8	Any other	12	13.3
9	Un married	4	4.4
	Total	90	100

Source: Survey data.

Participation in student politics

It is a fact that bureaucracy plays a crucial role in the socio-political development of the nation. In a democracy they have to function very closely with the political leadership. The development of relationship with them is largely the result of the political attitudes and values. In order to understand the political attitudes and perception of the bureaucracy an attempt is made to study their participation in student politics. Table III.15 shows that 22.2 percent of officers stated that they have participated in students' politics. 73.3 percent officers did not participate

Table III.15. Participation of IAS officers in student politics

Sl. No.	*Participation*	*No. of officers responded*	*Percent*
1	Participated	20	22.2
2	Not participated	66	73.3
3	No	4	4.4
	Total	90	100

Source: Survey data.

Table III. 16. Political affiliation of IAS officers during student politics

Sl. No.	*Name of the organization*	*No. of officers responded*	*Percent*
1	NSU (KSU)	6	6.6
2	SFI	1	1.1
3	ABVP	-	-
4	Any other	11	12.2
5	Not applicable	54	60
6	No response	18	20
	Total	90	100

Source: Survey data.

in students organizations and 4.4 percent did not respond to this question. This shows that these officers at a very young age had been tutored for a higher job in the society and this would aiso reveal the general tendency among the bureaucracy to be indifferent towards politics. Even those officers who had participated in student organizations and activities have mainly done it for the congress party and other liberal parties and their association with radical student groups was almost nil (table III.16 & 17). Perhaps this is why most of the bureaucrats show a hostile attitude towards radical politics and ideology. Their attitude towards political parties is also based on a particular value orientation. This also conditions their attitude towards coalition politics in Kerala. Table. III. 17 substantiates the indifferent attitude towards politics and political parties

Table III. 17. Political ideology of IAS officers in Kerala

Sl.No.	*Political party*	*No. of officers resonded*	*Percent*
1	Congress	9	10
2	Janata Dal	-	-
3	BJP	-	-
4	Left parties	1	1.1
5	Any other	2	2.2
6	No response	72	80
7	Not voted	5	5.5
8	Personal	1	1.1
	Total	90	100

Source: Survey data.

Reasons for Opting IAS as the Career

Table III. 18 indicate the factors contributed to the selection of IAS as the career. 66.6 percent of the officers agree that they opt for civil service due to career prospects, 5.5 percent opted for social status, 16.6 percent said it was a service, 5.5 percent for power and 1.1 percent chose it for salary and 3.3 percent have chosen IAS due to all the above reasons. A national level study conducted among the IAS probationers of 1992 batch reveals that 33.75 per cent of the probationers stated that diversity is the motivating factor for joining IAS. 31.25 percent officers said that it is challenging and 21.25 responded that status/prestige above all was the motivating factor[32].

Table III. 18. Reasons for Opting IAS as the Career

Sl. No.	*Reasons for opting the career*	*No. of officers responded*	*Percent*
1.	Career prospects	60	66.6
2.	Social status	5	5.5
3.	Service	15	16.6
4.	Power	5	5.5
5.	Salary	1	1.1
6.	All the above	3	3.3
7.	Any other	1	1.1
	Total	90	100

Source: Survey data.

Parents Attitude of IAS Officers

Regarding the parents attitude 87.7 per cent officers said that their parents attitude was encouraging, 12.2 percent said that their parents attitude was neither encouraging nor discouraging. One notable factor is that those officers' parents whose education is below matriculation and up to matriculation said that their parents attitude was neither encouraging nor discouraging.

In short the study reveals that the higher bureaucracy in Kerala in spite of higher literacy, political consciousness and radical socio-economic measures have adopted the attitudes and perceptions of its elite predecessors. This is largely because most of the civil servants belong to the recently urbanized educated strata of the rural rich in the Kerala countryside. Besides the upper class, the upper caste also finds adequate representation in the higher bureaucracy. Moreover, this rich background could also enable them to send their children to some of the best universities in the country. Through marriage alliances with their own colleagues and other political and elite business classes, the higher bureaucracy, like their counterparts elsewhere in the country strives to keep up the elite character of the bureaucracy. This social background in a way shapes and conditions their attitude and perception towards the question of equality and development. The result is that the bureaucracy which is committed to the ideals enshrined in the Indian constitution continues to preserves the colonial tradition and refuses to become a development oriented bureaucracy.

References

1. V. Subramaniam, *Social Background of India's Administrators*, New Delhi: Publication Division, Ministry of Information and Broadcasting, Government of India, 1971, p. 5.
2. Government of Kerala, *Indian Administrative Service-Gradation List of IAS officers*, Thiruvananthapuram: Government Press, 2001, 1994.
3. Padma Ramachandran. IAS, "Strengthening Democracy Through Empowerment of People", Seminar Conducted by Vakkom Moulavi Foundation Trust, Thiruvananthapuram: September 3, 1994 .
4. *Ibid.*
5. *Kerala Kaumudi*, January 13, 2001 A. Sreedhara Menon, *op. cit.*, p.321.
6. For more details see.
   (1) B.B. Mishra, *The Bureaucracy in India. A Historical Analysis of Development up to 1947,* New Delhi: Oxford University Press, 1977.
   (2) Sapru, R.K. *Civil Service Administration in India, New Delhi:* Deep & Deep Publications. 1985.
7. Mridul Eapen, *op. cit.*,p. 59.
8. T.N. Dhar, "Indian Administrative Service in Uttar Pradesh" in T.N. Chaturvedi (ed.), *Fifty Years of Indian Administration,* New Delhi: Indian Institute of Public Administration, 1999, p. 366.
9. V. Balakrishnan Nair, *op. cit.*,p. 42.
10. Ameer Ahammed Manappad, "Creamy Layer", *MES Bulletin*, August 2000, p. 5.* Two Buddhists mentioned their religion as 'Hindu'.
11. Adi. H. Doctor, "Administration for Development in India", *Indian Journal of Political Science*, Vol. XXXIX, January – March 1978, p.280.
12. M.V. Subbaiah Choudari, "Social Composition of Andhra Pradesh Bureaucracy: A Micro Level Study", *Indian Journal of Public Administration*, Vol. XXXVI, October – December 1994, p. 902.
13. B. Prasad, *Indian Administrative Service*, New Delhi: S. Chand & Co., 1968, p.106.
14. Rajendra Kumar and Kalpana Bhatnagar, "Background and Attitude of IAS Probationers of 1992 Batch and Faculty Members of LBS National Academy of Administration", *Administrator* Vol. XXIX, July – September1994, pp. 84-85.
15. Retna Bhattacharya, *Administrators in a Developing Society*, Bombay: Himalaya Publishing House, 1989, p.20.

16. B.R. Verma, *Bureaucracy and Administration – Studies in Policy, Performance and Reform,* New Delhi: Kanishka Publishers and Distributors, 1998, p. 62.
17. T.N. Dhar, *op. cit.*, p. 382.
18. *Ibid.*
19. Rajendra Kumar and Kalpana Bhatnagar, *op.cit.*, p. 85.
20. Retna Bhattacharya. *op.cit.*, p. 26.
21. *Ibid.*
22. R.K. Trivedi and D.N. Rao, "Regular Recruits to IAS - A Study", *Journal of National Academy of Administration,* Vol. 3, 1960, p. 34.
23. *India Today*, August 2001, p. 28.
24. Rajendra Kumar and Kalpana Bhatnagar, *op.cit.*, p. 72.
25. T.N. Dhar, *op.cit.*, p. 366.
26. Retna Bhattacharya, *op.cit.*, p. 28.
27. B.R. Verma, *op.cit.*, pp. 68-69.
28. T.N. Dhar, *op.cit.,* p. 366.
29. Retna Bhattacharya, *op.cit.,* p. 38.
30. B.R. Verma, *op.cit.,* p. 69.
31. Rajendra Kumar and Kalpana Bhatnagar, *op.cit.*, p. 73.
32. *Ibid.*

4

Role in Policy Formulation and Implementation

The policy formulation and implementation are the twin sovereign functions of any state. This is primarily a political function in the sense that it is always the political leadership who decides policies. It has always been the role of the bureaucracy to provide valuable inputs in the policy formulation. Moreover, it is one of the main roles of the bureaucracy to implement these policies thus formulated efficiently and effectively. In fact the success of a policy depends largely on its effective implementation. In short the role of the bureaucracy in these crucial function has been widely accepted in all political systems.

The concept of policy making was first formulated by the prominent political scientist Harold J. Lasswell in the 1950's. According to him "policy science is the study of the process of deciding, choosing and evaluating the relevance of all available knowledge for the solution of problems"[1]. Policy science is concerned with the contribution of systematic knowledge structured rationality and organised creativity for better policy making. Policy is a course of action in pursuit of a goal. Thomas R. Dey says that "public policy is whatever the government chooses to do or not to do"[2]. Public policy in some context refers to decisions about long range objectives or general directions of governmental action, which serves as guide to short run action in specific cases.

Public policies are made to carry out the best of a nation's goals, aims, intention and means for their realisation, which aims at the well being of the maximum number of people. Both making and execution of public policy are functional roles of all governmental and non-governmental actors[3]. Thus public policy is a proposed course of action of persons, groups or government with a given environment providing opportunities and obstacles within the policies, it proposed to utilise and overcome in an effort to reach a goal or realise an objective or perception[4].

In a democratic set up government is nothing but a reflection of the society as a whole. The government has various fields of operation like defence, education, health, finance etc. At the time of formulation of policies some objectives are determined which ought to be achieved at the end. In a parliamentary democracy like India the Union and State governments together with Cabinet and the Legislatures constitute the policy bodies. The sources of policy thoughts are diverse like political, economic or social. In some cases, the thoughts have emerged even from foreign influences[5]. According to a senior civil servant, "at the national level many policies are derived on the basis of compulsive influence of international agencies like World Bank and IMF in case of financial aid for projects. State plans are necessarily dependent on mobilisation of internal resources and devolution of central finances based on Finance Commission Report. In this circumstance policy decisions at state level and local level have only restricted scope"[=]. If we examine this we can see the role of bureaucracy and its close linkage with the advanced industrial countries and global institutions like IMF, World Bank etc[6]. The advanced industrial countries have started 'auditing' the policy framework of the Government of India. e.g. the issue of subsidy to the farm sector in India has ceased to a domestic problem of the Indian state. The international agencies and the advanced countries have strongly objected to the subsidies of the agricultural sector because it creates fiscal deficits in India and leads to bad management of the Indian economy. Thus the aid giving organizations influence the Indian economy[7]. It is alleged that the Kerala government had appointed a foreign consultancy, 'PDP Australia' to help to prepare budget guidelines, drafting of budget for 2002-03[8]. According to V. Ramachandran, IAS (Former Chief Secretary and Vice-Chairman, State Planning Board) the broad policies are framed by political leadership, which are concretaised through Planning Commission and National Development Council[9]. However, the role of higher bureaucracy is crucial at this stage. The broad policies are given substance by the bureaucracy through their rich experience and expertise. Public policy making in India is perhaps as polyarchal like other countries. The policy planning community in India is small, highly diverse and dispersed[10]. In the policy making process in India the following groups play an important role.Primarily political parties, intellectuals and experts are involved with these parties. Unfortunately, in India the political parties have never created their internal groups committed to develop their political action agenda. Political parties tend to galvanise into some policy search at the time of election. Neither any ruling national party nor the regional parties have thought it fit to develop their internal structure for development of policy agenda. At the time of election political parties work out some kind of manifesto, which are not taken seriously[11].

In a Parliamentary system, the Prime Minister at the national level and the Chief Minister at the state level emerge as the single most important policy actor. The parties, which come to power normally, take into account the promises it had made to the electorate at the time of election and attempt to make policies aimed at achieving those objectives. Policy making in India has to take place in the context of corruptive and variegated society. Society has its own variants, its own compulsions and its own dynamics. The ambitious goals set for society have put in a state of flux and change[12].

The bureaucracy in India was considered as the traditional source of policy thought and action[13]. After independence, with the emergence of party system the role had declined. While ministers take decisions, the bureaucracy takes the necessary action to implement them. However, the role of bureaucracy in policy making has grown its importance now a days. Both the policy formulation and the implementation roles of bureaucracy are so crucial that a number of policies are either done or not done at the bureaucratic level[14].

In some occasions the bill passed by the legislature become intentionally vague on certain issues allowing the higher bureaucracy a degree of discretion in implementing the policy[15]. At the same time the bureaucracy may find difficulties in implementing the policies without altering the intent of policy. In either case the bureaucracy play a crucial role in making and implementing policies[16].

Under the Indian Constitution the higher civil servants have a constitutional responsibility to advice on policy matters[17]. The official's advice on the financial and administrative implication of different policy alternates. Thus the higher bureaucracy, particularly the Secretary to the Government plays more than an advisory role in policy formulation[18].

The vast direct experience and knowledge enable the higher civil servants to argue from the positions of great strength about financial and administrative difficulties of policy proposals[19]. At the same time the political background of ministers does not train them in policy analysis. Most ministers come up with broad ideas of future policy, they have to depend on their official advisers for their transformation into concrete plans[20]. The position of the higher bureaucrats is further strengthened by his permanence in administrative organisation as compared to ministers. The majority of ministers want to devote greater attention to consideration of public policy, but is unable to do so because of their other commitments[21]. Thus the amount of delegation from politician to officials has greatly increased.

The implementation brings to play organisational structures, process and motivation. The mutual relationship between the administrators and politicians plays a crucial role. Implementation of policy requires working with many different groups, both governmental and non-governmental. In a parliamentary form of government the legislatures can influence policy implementation indirectly. Ministers head various departments of the government and higher and lower officials assist them in running the organisation. The legislatures exercise control over executives through parliamentary questions, adjournment motion, no-confidence motion etc[22]. The executive is answerable in the legislature about the measures of policy implementation.

In policy implementation, judiciary has a major role. It happens when the policy is not clearly worded and different interpretation of said policy is made. Here the court gives its verdict and whatever the court decides is normally considered[23]. The Judicial control over administration is an essential aspect. There has been a tremendous increase in the number of controversial administrative issues in Kerala. If a person feels that an official acted beyond the jurisdiction of area of authority, he can approach the court for review of justice. The process of administrative adjudication has made the governance more transparent.

Involvement of third parties in delivering of public service is an important aspect. It may appear that certain groups influence policies and its implementation. The departments often carry out their policies which these groups tell them to implement. Sometimes civil servants are having interest in their own particularly concerned with their own roles and plans. In such occasions court gives directions.

While implementing the policy the bureaucrats can exercise certain discretion[24]. A particular policy is associated with a series of subsidiary policies and guidelines at various point of time. In such occasions they can act according to their discretion. Such discretion and judgement may not be in accordance with the interests of major sections of society.

The annual financial statement of the country is an important instrument for interpreting policy at the operational level. The increasing power of business lobbies and closer link between ministers, senior policy making civil servants and businessmen gives increased cause for concern[25]. That is why C.P. Bhambhri commented, "The higher echelons of Indian bureaucracy were always integrated with the Indian capitalist classes. Indian bureaucracy believes in the fundamental social institution of private property and it has actively participated in managing state capitalist sector"[26].

The politico-administrative interference is one of the subject matters of this study. On the one hand we have demands for commitment from civil servants and on the other autonomy of administrators who are considered as politically neutral. Here the neutrality of the administrative apparatus is doubtful because commitment is more towards personalities rather than programmes. Late Rajiv Gandhi, the former Prime Minister of India commented the public mal-administration in the following words: "We have government servants who do not serve but oppress the poor and the helpless who do not uphold the law but convene with those who create the state and whole regions whose only concerns is their private welfare at the cost of the society"[27].

Many Senior IAS officers agree that their duty is to provide necessary information and to advice the ministers on decision making. However, civil servants complain that the ministers ignore the advises of these officials related to policies. At the same time many ministers including the Chief Minister complain that the IAS officers are not obeying the orders of the political executives.[28] Thus the exercise of policy making and policy implementation role of civil servants have evolved public criticism and top administrators in Kerala have faced an unusually serious challenge to their authority. The policy formulation, a complex process, in which local, national and global concerns are involved. The bureaucrats have their own consciously articulated value positions. They have their own emotions and interests and it is indeed a fact that both at the formulation and implementation level of public policies their biases creep in and distorts the policy decisions.

The role of policy formulation and implementation is crucial in the context of a unique Kerala model development. This is mainly because of the interventionist policy of the state, which called for an attitudinal change on the part of bureaucracy. An attempt is made here to examine, how far the Kerala civil servants contributed to this positive development, to what extend their training and orientation help them in this development and the factors responsible for this crucial change in attitude of bureaucracy. It is also imperative to examine the changing role of bureaucracy in the specific context of alternating coalition governments with distinct political ideology and socio-economic progarmmes. Moreover, the study also sought to examine, how far higher bureaucracy has been redefined its role in the context of democratic decentralization introduced by the LDF government in 1996.

Training of IAS Officers

Training is the process of developing skills, habits, knowledge and aptitudes in employees for the purpose of increasing the effectiveness of employees in their aptitudes for present government positions as well as preparing employees for future government positions[29]. A candidate before entering the civil service may have some technical/professional and other academic qualifications but it does not matter and he will be given proper training at the time of joining the service. The empirical data have revealed the fact that the training and orientation that they receive are adequate enough to discharge the responsibilities in the society. For instance, table. IV.1. shows that majority of civil servants are satisfied with the present training being imparted to them. 46.6 percent of the IAS officers responded that the training they received was good. Some 30 percent officers said that the training was very good, another 20 percent replied that the training they received was average and 3.3 percent responded that it was below average.

In a study of social background and attitude of the IAS probationers of 1992 batch, 46.67 percent responded that the training was highly rewarding where as the rest said that it had been satisfying. Regarding the training facilities at the academy, 66.67 percent responded that the overall facilities were excellent and another 33.33 percent

Table IV.1 Opinion of IAS officers in Kerala about the training they receive

Sl.No.	*Opinion about training*	*No. of officers responded*	*Percent*
1	Good	42	46.6
2.	Very good	27	30.0
3.	Average	18	20.0
4.	Below average	3	3.3
	Total	90	100

Source : Survey data.

said that the training was good. Some rated library facilities to be very poor.[30] According to them there are certain deficiencies in the training programme as well (see details[31]).

About the social and political environment on which 64.4 percent civil servants were of the opinion that the Kerala society is conducive to the proper and efficient working of administration (table IV.2). At the same time about 31 percent of them stated that it is not conducive to efficient working. They stated that there is a pervasive and strong political interference in the day today administration. Besides, some of the officials while agreeing with this point further added that the arrogance of the people had affected the smooth working of administration. According to them, it may be because of the deterioration in values, which had set in after independence by the predominance and overplay of politics in human affairs and has a general deterioration all around. This has affected the Kerala society also=.

The above observation of the higher civil servants about the socio-political environment of Kerala was rejected by some other officials who stated that they are conscious about the high level political awareness and literacy rate of the people. Their experience with Kerala society is different. This view was expressed by officers who hailed from other states, mostly from north India. According to them, "the Kerala society provided a proper environment and felt that they are working as if in their own state". They further stated that

Table IV.2 Opinion of IAS officers about Kerala society and culture which affect the smooth working of administration

Sl. No.	*Response of IAS officers*	*No. of officers responded*	*Percent*
1	Conducive	58	64.4
2	Not conducive	26	28.8
3	To a certain extent	2	2.2
4	Don't know	1	1.1
5	No response	3	3.3
	Total	90	100

Source: Survey data.

they never experienced any kind of discrimination. According to one north Indian senior officer "I feel more of an insider in Kerala than my own home state of Uttar Pradesh. I have enjoyed working in Kerala and have always told about this politician-administrator relationship to everybody at other state that I have come in contact with. In fact being an outsider has afforded me an opportunity of being totally objective and disinterested while taking decisions”=. Another officer responded that “arrogance of people had affected the smooth functioning of administration”. Similarly another officer also responded that “associated with every development activity there are problems”=. Majority of officers believe that Kerala society and culture have not affected the smooth working of bureaucracy.

Coalition Politics and Administration in Kerala

One important aspect of bureaucracy in Kerala has been that it has to work in the context of coalition politics. There have been debates about the relationship between coalition politics and development and while some people believe that coalition politics is functional to development others are of the opinion that it is dysfunctional. Whatever may be the merit of this debate it is generally believed that coalition politics indeed had affected the efficient working of administration and pursuing the goal of development. Coalition politics essentially involves sharing power and positions among its constituent units. Naturally this gives rise to a plethora of vested interests with disastrous effects on development and administration[32]. Table IV.3 reveals that overall

66.6 percent of them felt that coalition politics was destructive to development. However, about 22.2 percent respondents had a positive attitude towards coalition politics in the state. For example one official said, "I would say that coalition politics prevents concentration of political power. It helped to preserve a degree of administrative independence leading to administrative efficiency"=. The Hindu daily comments that, "the fact is that Kerala has a coalition government which is conducive to good governance. The pulls and pressures that operates are not styled by dominance of a single party. There has been a coalition government from the very inception and the bureaucracy has streamlined itself and operates largely independent of the politics in power. This might have contributed to the smooth functioning of the administration"[33].

Table IV. 3. Opinion of IAS officers about the influence of coalition politics in the administration of Kerala

Sl. No.	*Response of IAS officers*	*No. of officers responded*	*Percent*
1	Influencing	36	40
2	May be	24	26.6
3	No influence	20	22.2
4	Don't know	7	7.7
5	To a certain extent	3	3.3
	Total	90	100

Source: Survey data.

Continuation of colonial legacy

During the British days the functions of government were very limited. It was essentially related to the maintenance of law and order and keeping India open for British imperialism. It had limited developmental objectives. The chief executive officer, *Diwan* Sir. C.P. Ramaswami Iyer believed that discipline should be enforced with all its brutality if the bureaucracy were to acquire its credential as a vital organ of the government. The *Diwans*, encased the code of conduct in a steel frame which he himself had worked out. Promptness, punctuality and expediency marked its preferences. After independence the state of Travancore and Cochin passed into history and in this place the new Kerala state was borne on November 1, 1956. Contemporaneous with this transformation there also evolved a new bureaucracy. It has over the years become an organ of the political apparatus with loyalties divided between the countless political parties, which have sprouted like wild weeds.[34] The functions of the government has increased and multiplied and there is no single activity which the government deemed to interfere.

Table IV.4 shows that out of the 90 officers 27.7 percent responded that the legacy of colonial bureaucracy still persist, 53.3 percent responded that this is not be seen in the present day. About 17 percent responded that the possibility could be there and 2.2 percent said they did not know about it. According to one officer "the persistence of colonial legacy is rather weak, but surely it exists in many states of our country”=. Another officer

Table IV.4. Opinion of IAS officers about the continuation of colonial legacy

Sl. No.	*Response of IAS officers*	*No. of officers responded*	*Percent*
1.	Continuing	25	27.7
2.	Not continuing	48	53.3
3.	May be continuing	15	16.6
4.	Don’t know	2	2.2
	Total	90	100

Source: Survey data.

said that “society is like that, here the bureaucracy cannot be otherwise. The old concept of bureaucracy is workable to a certain extent. Civil servants have to work as per rules and concept laid down by political leaders or ministers in a democracy”=.

Table IV.5 shows that out of 90 respondents 74.4 percent officers responded that the present bureaucracy is development oriented. 22.2 percent said that bureaucracy is not development oriented. According to one senior officer “bureaucracy in Kerala has been more development oriented than it is in certain other states. It has also received adequate support from local pressure groups.There is no doubt that factorial pressure groups exist at the local level but these pressures have hardly succeeded in

Table IV.5. Opinion of IAS officers on development bureaucracy

Sl.No.	*Response of IAS officers about development bureaucracy*	*No. of officers responded*	*Percent*
1.	Development oriented	67	74.4
2.	Not development oriented.	20	22.2
3.	To a certain extent	2	2.2
4.	Not responded	1	1.1
	Total	90	100

Source: Survey data.

over-riding the basic development objectives”=. Another officer said “development should be left to local and individual initiatives”=. According to another officer “in Kerala, young IAS officers have no role in development” =.

Civil servants as agents of social change

Table IV.6 shows that out of the 90 officers 51.1 per cent officers responded that they are the agents of social change, 31.1 per cent officers said that they may be the agents of social change while 11.1 per cent believe that bureaucrats are not the agents of social change. 5.5 per cent responded that they couldn’t say. A good number of officers believe that “they can be the agents of social change and they should be so”=.

Table. IV.6. Response of IAS Officers about Civil Servants as the Agents of Social Change

Sl. No.	*Response of IAS officers*	*No. of officers responded*	*Percent*
1.	Agents of social change	46	51.1
2.	May be	28	31.1
3.	Not the agents of social change	10	11.1
4.	Cannot say	5	5.5
5.	Don't know	-	-
6.	Should be	1	1.1
	Total	90	100

Source: Survey data

Role in Policy Formulation

Figure IV.1. shows that out of the 90 officers 56.6 percent responded that they have active role in policy formulation. 31.1 percent said they have moderate role and 12.2 percent responded that they have no role at all. According to one senior officer "we are expected to be but not"=. Another officer responded "it is the job of senior civil servants to study policy options and present them to the minister. A civil servant's role demands more professionalism"=.

According to one senior IAS officer "policy decisions are mostly part of political agenda. These decisions are evolved from the election manifesto of the party in power. In case of coalition government as has usually been the case in Kerala, and now at the centre also, individual parties in the coalition set up evolve a common minimum programme" =. Some other officers had also expressed the same point of view. For instance according to another senior officer, "the ministers seldom show any interest in policies but on the contrary they are more inclined in postings, transfers and such individual cases"=. Similarly according to S.Guhan, a senior IAS officer, "ministers join the government with the notion that it is some kind of private property or a private limited company. They are seldom interested in policies. They are quite content to leave larger issues of policy to the bureaucracy"[35].

An important aspect in this connection is that the civil servants had not offered any creative criticism about the liberalization and privatization policies. The newspaper reports show that there have been very few debates or dissenting voices among the civil servants.[36] The entry of multinationals and the hefty pay and perks their executives get are cause for concern. They are only concerned with the expectation on the possibilities of liberalization such as postings abroad and career mobility, re-employment in international agencies and multinational companies after retirement.[37]

If we examine the election manifestoes of different political parties, policy differences among them are rather limited. The ideological level except where there is polarisation between the extreme right and left, the policies spectrum of

Fig. IV. 1 Response of IAS Officers about Their Role in Policy Formulation

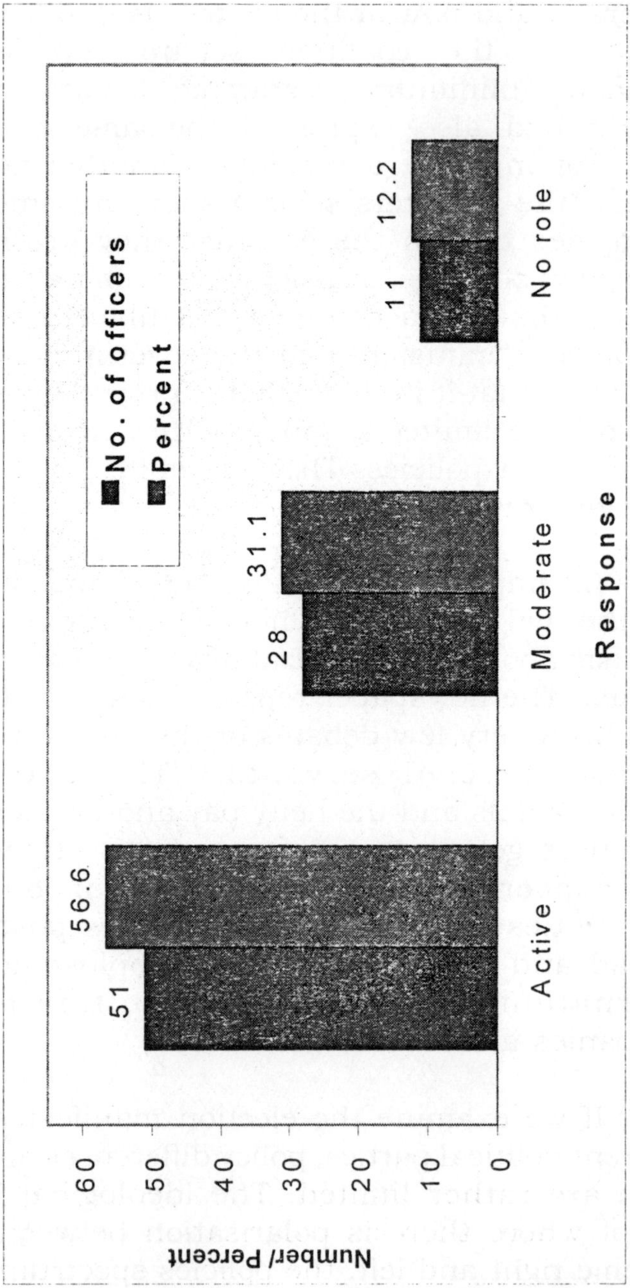

Source : Survey Data

parties like Congress (I), BJP, Janatha Dal and other regional parties have not much differences. The attitude of UDF and LDF on Asian Development Bank loan is a shining example in the recent times. This is due to the influence of international agencies both at the national and the state level.

Figure IV. 1. shows that 56.6 percent bureaucrats had responded that they have a major share in policy making. The junior officers in IAS like Sub Collector, Assistant Collector etc. said that they have no role in policy making. One officer made an interesting observation. According to him, "in the national and the state level there is not much differences between the policies of different parties of different coalition alliance. At the state level civil servants are told to implement them. In the states ministers and civil servants have only micro level or local level policy making. This type of policy formulation can hardly achieve any qualitative change in the lives of poor people"[=].

Suggestions Rendered by Bureaucrats in Favour of Politicians

The civil servants on the other hand do not always act in an independent, upright and fearless manner. Instead of giving free and frank advice to the political leadership at the policy formulation level their advice is structured in such a way as to suit the interests of the political leadership. About

43.3 percent of the officers expressed the same view (Figure. IV.2.). About 48.8 percent stated that the decisions are not tainted by political considerations. In this context it should be stated that the advices rendered by the bureaucracy have been influenced by short term political calculation. At least some officers are quite open and explicit in admitting that political considerations weigh heavily while making policy decisions. In this connection the observation of C.P. Bhambhri is quite appropriate. He stated that, "since the government is the chief regulator of the Indian economy, politico-bureaucratic decision makers exercise their power for protecting and promoting the interest of various competing classes in society and they also exercise this power for self advancement. During the last 50 years politico-bureaucratic strata of society have appropriated huge resources through their power of decision making. Politico-bureaucratic stratum exercised power to manage society and also maximise individual advantages for personal benefits".[38]

In the Kerala context also the political consideration in offering advices by the bureaucrats figure prominently. In many of the controversial policy decisions of the Kerala government during the 1990s both politicians and bureaucrats were involved. The data from vigilance sources have listed the cases like palm oil, graphite, land deed for Sanskrit University etc. The civil servants who give free and frank advice to administrator without fear or favour become unwanted. Corrupt politicians want civil servants

Fig. IV.2. Response of IAS Officers about Advice/Suggestions Offered by Civil Servants in Policy Matters to Suit the Interest of Politicians

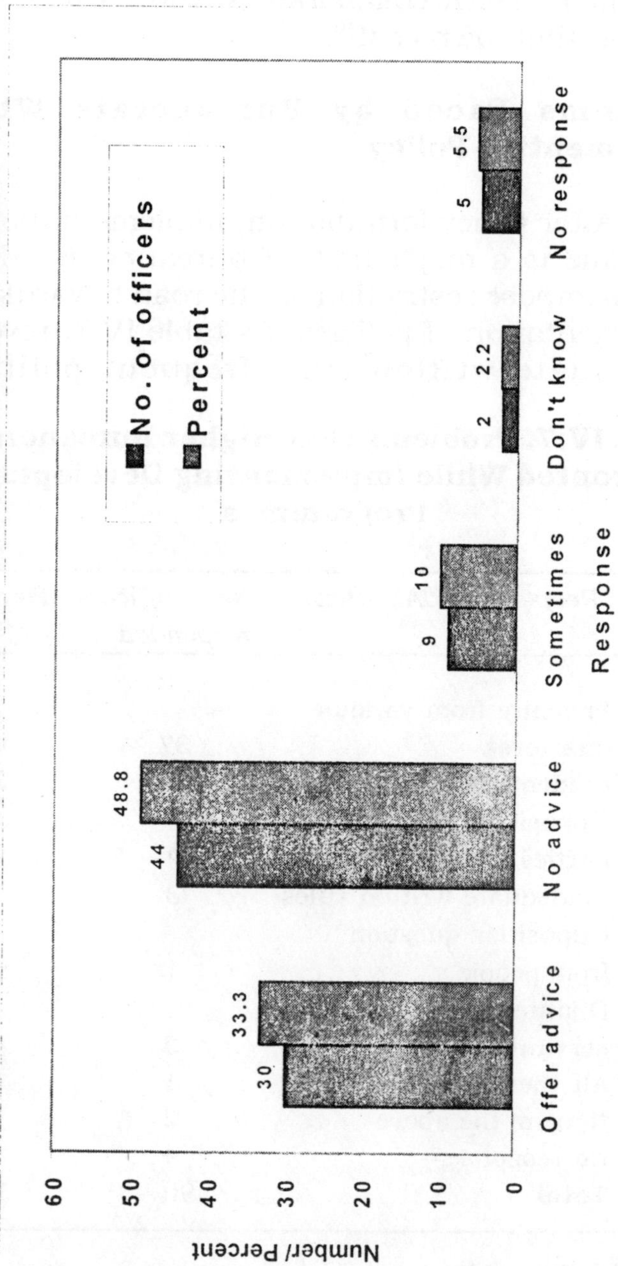

Source : Survey data.

to be their passive collaborators. Those who resist, do so at their own cost[39].

Problems Faced by Bureaucrats While Implementing Policy

After policy formulation, implementation of the same is a major task of bureaucracy. Many factors impose restriction on the road towards the implementation of policies. As table IV.7. reveals inadequate written rule, frequent political

Table IV.7. Problems that Higher Bureaucracy Confronted While Implementing Development Programmes

Sl. No.	*Response of IAS officers*	*No. of officers responded*	*Percent*
1.	Pressure from various quarters	37	41.1
2.	Inadequate finance	35	38.8
3.	Opposition from political parties & pressure groups	4	4.4
4.	Inadequate written rules	3	3.3
5.	Opposition question from people	1	1.1
6.	Disinterested government servants	3	3.3
7.	All these	1	1.1
8.	None of the above	2	2.2
9.	No response	4	4.4
	Total	90	100

Source: survey data

interference, lack of finance, pressures from vested interests, the disinterestedness of the civil servants and corruption are the major road blocks in the processes of implementation. In a coalition political setup, very few bureaucrats could act boldly against these pressures. Unlike other states the situation in Kerala is not that much hopeless. This was mainly due to the general awareness, infrastructural facilities and better communications.

It should be noted that the interpretation of rules governing the implementation is the prerogative of the higher bureaucracy. The interpretation of these rules may be objective or biased depending upon the character of bureaucrats. They distort these rules and make it ineffective in the context of pressures from various quarters. This happens invariably in almost all aspects of policy implementation. Political interference in policy implementation is the major reason to distort the rules to favour certain sections of the society. In the processes of policy implementation, higher bureaucrats and the state level civil servants maintain a friendly and co-opertive relationship despite their differing status in the hierarchically structured administration (table IV.8).

According to one senior officer from Uttar Pradesh, "Kerala is one of those states in which IAS officers do not have any major policy level conflicts with the state officer. The relationship has been largely harmonious and is based on strong foundation of mutual understanding of each others role and limitations. Both the agencies have taken a mature view of what they can expect from the others and have not taken each other for granted"

Table IV. 8. The Relationship Between the Higher Civil Servants and the Lower Level State Staff

Sl. No.	*Response of IAS officers*	*No. of officers responded*	*Percent*
1.	Excellent	22	24.4
2.	Good	49	54.4
3.	Fair	17	18.8
4.	Poor	—	—
5	Depends	1	1.1
6.	Don't know	1	1.1
	Total	90	100

Source: Survey data

Intervention of political leaders at the district level

At the district level the collector is the principal agency through which the policies get implemented. The developmental activities at the district level are co-ordinated by the collector. Naturally, there will be tremendous pressure in his administrative functions. Local political leadership and other influential sections of the society could be exerting pressures on the collector to implement policies in such a fashion so as not to harm their interests. Naturally the question arises at this juncture is how many officers have the courage and conviction to stand against the pressure from these quarters? As the table IV.9. shows about 62 percent officers admitted that they are under tremendous pressure from politicians and rich sections while working at the district level. In order to be effective in implementation, he should have sufficiently longer tenure in the districts. Frequent transfers and changes at the crucial level of administration are to be avoided. Effective implementation of policies as the study shows was hampered by frequent political interferences. Besides political interference, other factors like caste, money power and business interests indeed exert tremendous pressures on administration. According to one officer who is in the rank of Chief Secretary "the pseudo-secular community pretending to engage in social upliftment is a major menace to people's well being in Kerala and act as a great stumbling block to proper administration" =. Another senior officer also responded like this, for him "the political resistance as such is not that much political because from my experience it is seen that it is the class caste interest that is into political resistance."= This is clear from table IV.9. At the same time, table IV.10 shows that there exists a reasonable level of interaction of bureaucrats with district, block and village level political leadership and the quality of these

Table IV.9. Bureaucracy and Unfair Intervention by Political Leaders

Sl. No.	*Response of IAS officers*	*No. of officers responded*	*Percent*
1.	Often	42	46.6
2.	Very often	14	15.5
3.	Rarely	30	33.3
4.	Never	—	—
5	No opinion	3	3.3
6.	Depends	1	1.1
	Total	90	100

Source : Survey data.

Table IV.10. Bureaucracy's Level of Interaction with District, Block and Village Level Political Leaders

Sl. No.	*Response of IAS officer*	*No. of officers responded*	*Percent*
1.	Often	38	42.2
2.	Very often	33	36.6
3.	Rarely	16	17.7
4.	Not so	1	1.1
5	No response	1	1.1
6.	Don't know	1	1.1
	Total	90	100

Source: Survey data.

interactions mainly depends upon the nature of officers. Some officers have maintained continuous interaction with their political counterparts. For instance according to one senior officer "I visited almost every village in my subdivision at least once in two months. By the end of the sixth month, I knew all the revenue defaulters in the district. My visit to village offices was informed in advance so that people could come and see me".[40] In other words proper implementation of the developmental policies at the district level demands a co-operative and friendly interaction between political and administrative leadership at the district level. However, one officer rightly draws the proper relationship between the two functionaries. According to him "From the very nature of the two functionaries one with personal short term ambitions and the other having impersonal long term perspectives, some conflict is inevitable. We should not therefore, expect a totally smooth interaction. Occasional conflicts do take place and eventually it gets resolved. But the civil servants should make their stand clear from the very beginning"[=].

Opinion of Bureaucrats about Democratic Decentralisation

Since the introduction of Panchayati Raj system under the 73rd Constitutional Amendment Act by which certain powers had been transferred to the grass root level from the state government. These bodies have been empowered to play a positive and creative role in the formulation and implementation of development scheme at the grass root level[41]. Majority of the officers have recognized this role (table IV.11 &12). Thus there is an attitudinal change on the part of bureaucracy towards democratic decentralization. At the same time, in fact some of the officers were very positive when they stated that the developmental policies should evolve from the people that is at the grass roots level. In short the developmental dimension of the Panchayati Raj system was appreciated by almost everyone. According to V. Ramachandran, Chairman of the Committee on Decentralisation observed "even after the implementation of the Panchayti Raj system the decentarlisation of

Table IV.11. Opinion of IAS Officers about the Limited Achievements of Democratic Decentralisation

Sl. No.	*Response of IAS officers*	*No. of officers responded*	*Percent*
1	Fully agree	20	22.2
2	Partially agree	50	55.5
3	Partially disagree	10	11.1
4	Fully disagree	6	6.6
5	No response	3	3.3
6	Don't know	1	1.1
	Total	90	100

Source: Survey data

powers has not materialized"[42].A detailed study of several panchayats in Kerala indicated that the objective of decentarlisation and people's planning for rural development was materialized to a limited extent. In the implementation of developmental measures there is large scale corruption and favouritism. This is due to age old traditional outlook and caste communal and political favouritism[43].

Table IV.12. Opinion of IAS officers about the effectiveness of Panchayati Raj in achieving its goals

Sl. No.	*Response of IAS officers*	*No. of officers responded*	*Percent*
1	Fully agree	16	17.7
2	Partially agree	38	42.2
3	Partially disagree	19	21.1
4	Fully disagree	6	6.6
5	No response	9	10
6	To a certain extent	2	2.2
	Total	90	100

Source: Survey data

Regarding the effectiveness of Panchayati Raj institutions, about 60 percent of officers are appreciative of the positive role played by elected members in policy formulation, planning, priority determination etc. (table. IV.12.). But in actual practice the power has not been devolved to Panchayati Raj Institutions. According to one officer "There is need for mature, co-ordinated efforts. This is possible only if all political parties sit down together and make a realistic assessment of the benefits that would achieve. The establishment of people's rapport between officials and non- official is a principal pre-condition for the desired objectives in rural areas"=.

Table IV.13. Response of IAS Officers about the People's Impression about Administrative Inefficiency in Government

Sl. No.	*Response of IAS officers*	*No. of officers responded*	*Percent*
1	Fully agree	43	47.7
2	Partially agree	43	47.7
3	Partially disagree	4	4.4
4	Fully disagree	-	-
	Total	90	100

Source: Survey data

Another important point that emerges in the course of the study is the efficiency in administration of developmental policies. The study clearly establishes the fact that various factors mentioned earlier critically affects the administrative efficiency. Majority of the officers studied have shared the feeling of common people that there exists widespread inefficiency in administration (table IV.13), which has certainly hampered proper and effective implementation of developmental policies.

Although, the Kerala culture is conducive for the smooth functioning of bureaucracy, the political pressure exerted on them makes the platform more dysfunctional. Recently the policy formulations, which are supposed to make drastic changes in the life of ordinary people, are by and large influenced by international agencies. All emphasizes the need for a new administrative culture. The new culture should be grounded in efficiency, transparency and commitment to the people.

References

1. Harold J. Lasswell, "Policy Sciences", *International Encyclopaedia of Social Sciences*, Vol. 12, New York: MacMillan, 1968, p. 20.
2. Thomas R. Dey, *Understanding Public Policy*, London: Prentice Hall, 1978, p. 56
3. Alfred C.Tandau, *Policy Implementation in India*, New Delhi: Vikas Publication, 1996, p. 98.
4. *Ibid*, p. 99.
5. C.P. Bhambhri, *op. cit.*,p.210.* Interview data.
6. *Ibid*, p. 219.
7. *Ibid.*
8. *The New Indian Express*, February 13, 2002.
9. V. Ramachandran, *Bureaucracy*, Proceedings of the Symposium Conducted by Financial Express, Thiruvananthapuram: Printed by the Kerala State Land Use Board, October 6, 1986, p.20.
10. V.A. Pai Panandikar, *Policy Sciences and Policy Making in India*, New Delhi: Centre for Policy Research, 1988, p.25.
11. *Ibid.*
12. Alfred C. Tandau, *op. cit.*, p.68.
13. V.A. Pai Panandikar, *op. cit.*,p.25.
14. R.K. Sapru, *op. cit.*,p.156.
15. Robert B. Denhardt and Barry H. Hammond, *Public Administration in Action, Readings, Profile and Cases*, California: Border Pacific, 1992, p.46.
16. *Ibid*, p.46.
17. R. K. Sapru, *op. cit.*, p.157.
18. *Ibid.*
19. *Ibid.*
20. V. Ramachandran, *Bureaucracy*, *op. cit.*, pp. 6-7.
21. R.K. Sapru, *op. cit.*,p. 157.
22. Alfred C. Tandau, *op. cit.*,p.111.

23. *Ibid.*
24. Robert B. Denhardt & Barry H. Hammond, *op. cit.,* p. 46.
25. *Ibid,* p.146.
26. C.P. Bhambhri, *The Indian State- Fifty Years, op.* cit., p. 219.
27. Cited by N.C. Saxena, "Administration and the People- Higher Bureaucracy Needs for Radical Reforms", *Management in Government*, Vol. XXXII No. 3, October- December, 2002, p. 3.
28. *Kerala Kaumudy*, January 11, 2002.
29. Dale Earnest, *Management Theory and Practice*, Tokyo: Mac Graw-Hill, 1973, p.375.
30. Rajendra Kumar and Kalpana Bhatnagar, *op. cit.*, p 85.
31. *Ibid. a) Insufficient testing of instruments, methodology development, research and consultancy. b) Guest faculty often provide inputs about what they know rather than what is relevant. C) Training should be more practical oriented. d) More of laws, language, competence, case studies and tutorials should be there and lectures should be reduced. e) Short term nature of the faculty does not encourage and the faculty should be highly accountable, innovative and responsive to the changing needs. Short term dominates over long range planning. It is fôr these reasons that inputs are not upto standard and are faculty- based rather than need- based. f) Horse riding is expensive and irrelevant with out much merit, at best a lobby with glamorous value and g) Insufficient interaction among the probationers outside the classroom.*
   - Interview data
   - Interview data
   - Interview data
32. K. Sadanandan, "Politicisation of the Bureaucracy", *The Hindu*, March 24, 1992.
33. *Ibid.*
34. *Ibid.*
   - Interview data
   - Interview data
   - Interview data
   - Interview data
35. S.Guhan, "*Bureaucracy*", *op. cit.,* p. 12.
36. P.J. Alexander, "Role of the Civil Service in the Context of the New Economic Policy", *Kerala Journal of social science*, Vol. I, No.1, January–June 1996, p. 139.
37. *Ibid.*
   - Interview data
38. C.P. Bhambhri, *op. cit.*, pp. 168-169.

39. P.R. Dubhashi, "Restructuring and Reform of Indian Political Administrative and Economic System" in T.N. Chaturvedi (ed.) *Fifty Years of Indian Administration, op. cit.,* p.107.
   - Interview data
40. K.J. Alphons, *Making a Difference,* New Delhi: Viking Publishers, 1996, p. 15.
   - *Interview data*
41. Details see,
   1) *Kerala Panchayati Raj Act 1994*, Thiruvananthapuram: Government Press, 1994.
   2) *Kerala Municipality Act 1994*, Thiruvananthapuram: Government Press, 1994.
42. *Kerala Kaumudi,* November 24, 2000.
43. *The New Indian Express,* September 7, 2000.
   - Interview data

5

The Relationship between Bureaucrats and Politicians

In this chapter the relationship between bureaucrats and politicians has been discussed mainly on the basis of interview data. The attitude and perception of about 90 higher civil servants from the state cadre and about 50 political functionaries like ministers, former ministers, local body members and party leaders were collected on the basis of a structured questionnaire. While the interview schedule used for obtaining data from higher civil servants were mainly based on a closed questionnaire, the questionnaire used for politicians was an open ended one. This is mainly because of the need for detailed answers from the politicians on various questions. Unlike the politicians the higher civil servants were comparatively more co-operative in answering the questions.

vested interests. This nexus causes a drain on public treasury. In recent times the bureaucrats were also criticised for almost everything like rising prices, crime, deforestation, indifference and insensitivity to public grievances and developmental failures[7]. At no time in the past that so many senior bureaucrats face criminal procedure and corruption enquiries. Almost every political leader regardless of party affiliation blames bureaucracy for his own failure and calls for greater political control over it[8].

Thus the relation between the politicians and bureaucrats are very delicate. In Kerala no tradition have so far been developed to put them on an enduring basis. The relation should be examined from various angles disregarding on particular considerations.

Relationship between Bureaucrats and Politicians

An analysis of the survey data from the higher bureaucrats clearly reveals their relationship with politicians by and large positive. More than 70 percent of the respondents stated that generally there exists a good relationship. However, 22.2 percent officers said that the relationship is not so good (table V.1). One officer responded that "vested interests, if both are neutral no problems"= and another officer responded that "good with decent politicians and not so good with indecent politicians".=

Table V.1. Opinion of IAS Officers about the Relationship between Bureaucrats and Politicians

Sl. No.	*Response of IAS officers*	*No. of IAS officers responded*	*Percent*
1	Excellent	4	4.4
2	Good	61	67.7
3	Not so good	20	22.2
4	Don't know	1	1.1
5	Depends	3	3.3
6	No response	1	1.1
	Total	90	100

Source: Survey data.

One important factor, which affects the morale of the civil service, is the interference of the ministers and other politicians in the day to day administration on behalf of their party workers, friends and relatives. Such interference may lead to bending of rules and regulations. Regarding the question on interference of politicians in the day to day administration, 80 percent of the respondents agree that it hampers administrative efficiency (figure V.1). About 11.1 percent officers said that though political interference takes place it wouldn't affect the efficiency. A senior civil servant commented, "In any system interference from outside hamper the efficiency."=

According to V. Ramachandran, a former Chief Secretary "every minute of their lives they

Fig. V.1. Opinion of IAS Officers about Political Interference in Administration

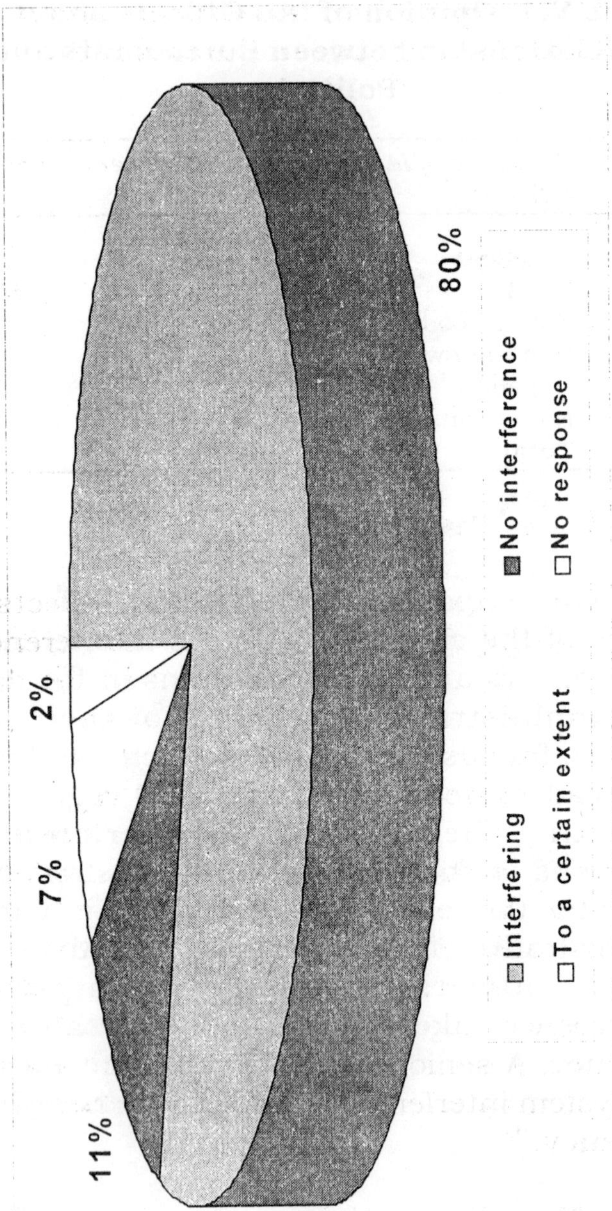

Source: Survey data

Fig. V. 2. Response of IAS Officers about the Influence of Personal, Ideological and Political Considerations in the Transfer of IAS Officers

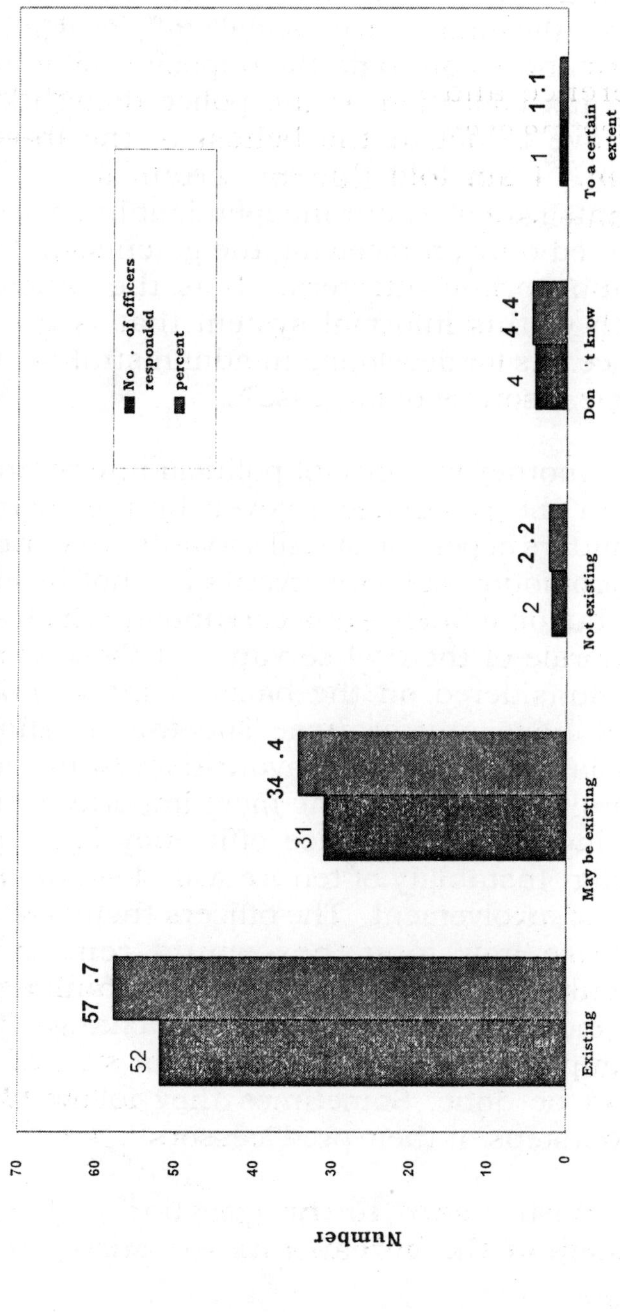

Source: Survey data

are under intense pressure from the informal system - the minister's personal staff, local political leaders and so on to do the opposite. Whether it is the tax collection or the police doing its job, you have to act at the behest of the informal system. I am told that in certain states even warrants issued by our independent judiciary will be served only on receiving the green signal from the appropriate quarters. It is the cancerous growth of this informal system that is the true menace. As for development administration it has become a source of largesse"[9].

Another instance of political interference is seen in the patronage enjoyed by politicians in the matters of posting of civil servants. The transfer and promotion of civil servants are not based on merit but on influence and corruption, which affect the morale of the civil servants. If these matters were considered on the basis of merit, nobody would have any grouse. The fact is that all politicians like to show favouritism to particular officers[10]. Thus one of the most important malice affecting the civil service efficiency is frequent transfer. Instability of tenure will lead to lack of sense of involvement. The officers themselves are not sure how long they would remain in a particular post. This affects their thinking and even incrementally about how to change things and improve them and they are not sure of what should be done. Sometimes they follow blindly the footsteps of their predecessors[11].

With regard to the question of frequent transfers of the bureaucrats the survey reveals that more than 57.7 percent of the bureaucrats stated that personal ideological and political considerations outweigh all other matters in this regard (figure. V.2). It is a fact that transfer policy has been used as an instrument of reward and punishment. Transfer from one post to another after a short stay is considered as a stigma. This is mainly because the officer on transfer does not get his position defended publicly on restrictions in service rules. Moreover, the higher officials are transferred to junior positions almost as a punishment. Even this policy will affect their efficiency because they do not get an opportunity to have a thorough understanding of the problem of the department.

A study conducted on transfer policy of IAS officers in Uttar Pradesh reveals that average tenure of officials in the last 5 years is less than 6 months[12]. In Kerala it is widely noticed that higher civil servants are changed with every change in the political leadership. This applies to both LDF and UDF governments. For instance in 1996, the CPM-led (LDF) coalition government and in 2001 the Congress-led (UDF) coalition governments have made thorough changes in the higher echelons of bureaucracy immediately after assuming office[13]. Similarly, when a new government assumes office in the state, top officers as well as Chairmen and the Managing Directors of public sector undertakings are also get changed. Each political party in power has its own set of favourite officials. Such officers are re-appointed in prestigious public positions with high salary and perks after retirement (details see)[14].

If the administration is to work efficiently and smoothly, and the objectives of the government and well being of the people are to be properly achieved, the ministers and his officials in the ministry must work with co-operation and harmony. There is no denying the fact that efficiency and good governance would largely depend upon the good relationship between the politicians and bureaucrats. This study also reveals that the bureaucrats have always tried to please the political leadership for obvious reasons. For instance nearly 58.8 percent of the officials agreed to this trend. However, 18.8 percent of the officials did not agree with this stand and 22.2 percent of the officers very cleverly did not answer the question (table V.2).

Table V.2. Tendency of IAS Officers not to Displease the Politicians

Sl. No.	*Response of the IAS officers*	*No. of officers responded*	*Percent*
1	Not to displease	53	58.8
2	Displease	17	18.8
3	Don't know	20	22.2
	Total	90	100

Source: Survey data.

It should be noted that this tendency of not to displease the politicians was not there in the early years of post-independent India but since then it had become a common phenomenon. T.N. Seshan's (former Chief Election Commissioner of India) view is that "the number of bureaucrats who would confront with politicians is going down fast because every one is trying to feather his own nest. Unless a man is mentally off, he would not try to confront a politician. Bureaucrats suffered from a basic loss of character. The traditional civil service value and neutrality and integrity are no longer relevant"[15].

Major Areas of Conflict between Bureaucrats and Politicians

There are many areas of conflicts between politicians and bureaucrats. These include the policy formulation, strategic level and implementation level. Nearly 78.8 percent of the respondents stated that policy implementation stage is the main area of conflict. Only 13.3 percent officers mentioned that conflict also arises at the policy formulation stage (table V.3). According to N.S. Jagannathan, "the relationship between the politicians and the bureaucrats has deteriorated to a point where the civil servants are not able to perform his legitimate functions. Political interference and pressure, necessity to collect money for the party and for oneself to fight the next election, changes in the political culture" etc. are some of the reasons for this[16]. P.S Appu (former Director of the Lal Bahadur Sastri National

Table. V.3. Major Areas of Conflict between IAS Officers and Politicians

Sl. No.	*Response of IAS officers*	*No. of IAS officers responded*	*Percent*
1	Policy formulation	12	13.3
2	Strategic level	2	2.2
3	Implementation level	71	78.8
4	All the above	2	2.2
5	No conflict	2	2.2
6	Nil	1	1.1
	Total	90	100

Source: Survey data.

Acadamy of Administration), states, "Our plans have become more and more sophisticated and our implementation has become poorer and poorer. The planning process itself has been getting more and more refined from plan to plan from the Second Plan. But the implementation has been getting worse. All over the place corruption has become rampant. I do not think that the senior bureaucracy is a helpless spectator in this. I am of the view that by and large they are active collaborators"[17].

It is interesting to note that 75 percent of the higher officials narrated their personal experience of confrontation with political leadership (table V.4). In almost all cases the government officials had adopted a compromising attitude for their own interests. The main reasons for this is that every issue got politicised and a conscientious civil servant who takes an independent position does not get support from the politicians or from their own colleagues. This trend would degenerate into indifference and inaction on the part of civil servants affecting even their morale.

Another interesting tendency among the bureaucrats is that they invariably adopt a policy of offering advices and suggestions by taking into account the interest of politicians. This is quite unfortunate because the bureaucrats are

Table V.4. Experience of IAS Officers on Confrontation with Politicians.

Sl. No.	*Response of IAS officers*	*No. of IAS officers responded*	*Percent*
1	There is confrontation	67	74.4
2	No confrontation	20	22.2
3	To a certain extent	1	1.1
4	No response	2	2.2
	Total	90	100

Source: Survey data.

supposed to provide independent advice to the politicians. According to C.P. Bhambhri, "since the government is the chief regulator of the Indian economy their power for protecting and promoting the interest of the various competing classes in society and they also exercises this power for self advancement. During the last 50 years politico-bureaucratic strata of society have appropriated huge resources through the power of decisionmaking. Politico- bureaucratic stratum exercises power to manage society and also maximises individual advantages for personal benefits"[18].

In Kerala many cases have been reported involving politicians and bureaucrats, for example: palm oil deal, graphite case, Sanskrit University land deed etc. are only some of them. Thus it is a fact that corrupt politicians want civil servants to be their collaborators. The means used to bend civil servants to minister's will are arbitrary use of the power of transfer, out of turn promotion, arbitrary suspension and institution of enquiry. Shameful acts of victimisation of honest and unpliable civil servants do takes place. The cases shown below clearly illustrate the issue.

1. **Graphite case:** In this sensational case which deals with selling of electricity to a private firm in Bangalore through Karnataka State Electricity Board. The Vigilance Court, Thiruvananthapuram found the then Kerala Electricity Minister, R. Balakrishna Pillai and the KSEB Chairman P. Kesava Pillai responsible in the deal. The main allegation was that the minister sold electricity to a private firm in his personal interest without the knowledge of the ministry[19]. The Vigilance Court verdict was one year imprisonment and Rs. 10,000 penalty to the minister and the KSEB Chairman. The High Court of Kerala uphold

the verdict of the Vigilance Court. The court also severely criticised the then Power Secretary G. Gopalakrishna Pillai. The case is now pending in the Supreme Court.

2. **Sanskrit University land deed**: In acquiring land for the Thiruvananthapuram centre of the Sanskrit University, the Vigilance Court, found R. Ramachandran Nair IAS, former Chief Secretary and Ex-Vice Chancellor of the University guilty. While acquiring the land, the University had paid 10 times more than the actual cost of the land causing a loss of about 33 lakh to the government. The court slapped a 3 years imprisonment and Rs. 50,000 penalty on him[20].

3. **Palm oil deal**: The Comptroller and Auditor General of India (CAG) in his Report for the year ended March 31, 1993 has examined the irregularity and impropriety in the import of 15,000 tonnes of palm oil from a Singapore based Company. Based on this report a criminal case was filed before the Deputy Superintendent of Police (Vigilance), Thiruvananthapuram against 1) K. Karunakaran, then Chief Minister of Kerala, 2) S. Padmakumar, then Chief Secretary of Kerala, 3) Directors of Power and Energy Pvt. Ltd., Singapore, 4) Director of Mala Export Corporation at Madras etc[21]. The court found K. Karunakaran and S. Padmakumar guilty. Presently the issue is pending before the High Court of Kerala.

The study also shows that the political leadership invariably manipulates the administrative decisions to suit the interest of their party, community and the regions. In this situation 80 percent of the civil servants expressed their inability to do anything against the decisions of political leadership (table V. 5). This clearly shows that majority of the civil servants have lost their will to fight against gross political interference and injustice. This is mainly because the civil servants themselves often manipulate decisions to suit the interest of their fellow beings. N.S Jagannathan confirms this fact in his words, "One hears horrendous stories about corruption, nepotism and favouritism involved even in such things as securing seats in professional colleges in which ministers and even chief ministers take a personal interest"[22].

Table V. 5. Tendency of Political Leadership to Manipulate Administrative Decisions for Parochial Ends

Sl. No.	*Response of IAS officers*	*No. of IAS officers responded*	*Percent*
1	True	72	80
2	False	6	6.6
3	To a certain extent	5	5.5
4	No response	6	6.6
5	Nil	1	1.1
	Total	90	100

Source: Survey data.

Examples of manipulation of administrative decisions by politicians and civil servants are galore in Kerala. For instance the blatant ministerial interference in the Kerala Medical Entrance Examination of 2001 was widely debated. A court case was filed against the Education Minister about this issue in the High Court of Kerala. The final verdict is yet to come[23]. However, the case has certainly exposed the character and integrity of the political leadership. The interesting aspect of this case is that the Minister has shown blatant community favouritism to a Muslim candidate to get through the selection processes. The Entrance Commissioner to whom the Minister asked for favour refused to oblige, and as a consequence this upright senior civil servant was punished by transferring to an insignificant post.

This case has indeed exposed the corrupt nature of political leadership. The reason for this is that politics of the country has become divorced from public welfare and it is more concerned with narrow sectarian interests. The political leaders think that electoral outcome can be manipulated through caste or other populist means at the time of election. To contest election requires massive amounts of money, which is collected through shabby deals. The opinion of C. Subramaniam, former Union Minister is significant. He says: "Now a days, as soon as the party comes to power, the first thought is about how to collect money for the next election. So, throughout the tenure in office, a major objective is to secure adequate financial resources to face the next election. It therefore becomes the responsibility to every minister to gather as much money as possible from his department. The whole system has got corrupted in this manner. Once this becomes the main preoccupation, administration suffers. Decision becomes subjective and not objective. Inevitably the bureaucracy has to play a willing or unwilling role in this process"[24]. As a consequence the civil servant's neutrality and commitment has become the casuality. It is in this context the various developmental policies are formulated and implemented. As a result the implementation of developmental policies becomes tardy.

In this context, the higher civil servants instead of providing independent advice often tend to yield to political pressure. At times in order to save their face they record their objections in the same file and wait for and abide by the ministers decision. Thus the politicians instead of encouraging the civil servants to act honestly and uprightly compel to show political conformity in their decision. It is a fact that the higher bureaucracy has almost surrendered their professional ethics and moral integrity to the politicians.

In Kerala, where coalition governments have been in power, the relationship between politicians and bureaucrats has become murkier. In this context it should be noted that certain upright officers in the Kerala cadre who tried to interpret rules in a fair and objective manner, often come into conflict with political leadership. Even though they belong to a minority category their independent interpretation of rules should be encouraged. The ministers, instead of encouraging such officers, adopt a policy of punishing them by frequent transfer from one department to another. The attitude of political leadership towards bureaucracy would ultimately demoralise the entire administration. For instance, some of the upright officers like Raju Narayana Swami, K.J. Alphons, Sukumar N. Oommen etc. were transferred on account of having adopted an independent stand. One may come across many such cases in the annals of Kerala administrative history. In order to illustrate this, the cases of K.J.Alphons, Sukumar N. Oommen and Raju Narayana Swami are cited below.

1. K.J. Alphons, an upright IAS officer who always takes strong independent decisions had been victimised by frequent transfers to junior posts. He was transferred from the post of Transport Secretary to the Entrance Commissioner, since he did not allow the interference of the Transport Minister in the transfer of employees under him. As the Entrance Commissioner, he implemented many policies for the efficient functioning of the department much to the dislike of the existing bureaucratic culture. He was therefore, transferred to a lower post as Land Use Commissioner. This action has taken since, he did not obey the request of

the Education Minister Nalakathu Soopy to replace the income certificate of a candidate for Kerala Medical Entrance Examination with another certificate showing less income. The new certificate would enable the candidate to exempt himself from the creamy layer in seeking admission to MBBS[25].

2. Sukumar N. Oommen, another upright IAS officer was transferred from the post of Chairman, Kerala State Electricity Board, for disclosing the illegal attempt to purchase power from Ennore Power Project in Tamilnadu. The plan for the purchase has been made upon the directive from the then Electricity Minister, S.Sarma violating the policy of the government to purchase cheapest power[26].

3. Raju Narayana Swami, an IAS topper had to face much hardship including suspension from service due to political pressure. He was transferred from the post of Thrissur District Collector by a simple fax message. The reason apparently was he stood firm on revenue recovery. Later he was transferred from the post of Kasargod Collector to Employment Director. The reason he alleges was that, he did not write a favourable report for obtaining approval for a paramedical course in a hospital without any facilities. It is reported that the hospital belongs to a Minister's

daughter. According to this popular officer "all frequent transfers I faced are due to the fact that I did not support corruption. I have never yielded to any political pressure and has taken any decision against the larger interests of the government and the public"[27].

Opinion of the Politicians

After examining the bureaucratic attitude towards politicians, it is imperative to understand how political leadership perceive the role of bureaucracy in a democratic set up. There is no doubt that political leadership occupies an important position in any democratic political set up. Similarly the role of bureaucracy is clearly defined in a political system. But the frequent political changes with a distinct ideology and socio-economic programme, the bureaucracy has to play a very difficult and conflicting political and administrative role. The higher bureaucracy, by and large, has redefined their role to suit the changing socio-economic milieu. The bureaucracy has itself recognised the commanding role of political leadership in the decision making process. It is in this context the attitude of politicians towards higher bureaucracy is analysed.

The respective role of politicians and bureaucrats in the decision making process has been a much debated issue in the administrative behaviour. So the study also confirms the general notion that the political leadership invariably plays a dominant role in the decision making process. More than 60 percent of the politicians have affirmed their position (survey data). However, about 40 percent of the respondents stated that both politicians and bureaucrats are equal partners in the decision making process. This is because decision-making process involves the crucial inputs from both these sections. That is to say policies are actually considered by the political leadership with inputs and experience provided by the bureaucrats.

Similarly on the question of the class nature of higher bureaucracy, more than 65 percent of the political leadership stated that a colonial mindset continued to be dominant in the behavioural pattern of bureaucracy and has not yet become development oriented, despite various reform attempts. A political leader observes "the attitude of higher bureaucracy has changed only to a certain extent. During the colonial period the concept of development administration had limited scope. After independence, the bureaucracy to a certain extend become development oriented but their attitude towards common man is not changed"[28].

About the commitment of the bureaucracy towards the policies of the government and especially on the question of effective implementation of these policies, majority of the political leaders interviewed by the researcher have expressed their view that bureaucracy's commitment to development is very low, that is only 25-30 percent.

According to a senior minister who occupied important ministerial positions in various governments since 1957, "there are committed bureaucrats as well as a few who follow the implementation in a mechanical manner. It depends upon the ability and performance of the minister. Implementation of the policies is mainly done by the lower level officials worked out by the higher bureaucrats"[29]. The Chief Minister of Kerala, A.K. Antony made a critical observation about higher civil servants in Kerala. "The IAS officers in Kerala are not committed to their duty. They are not presenting an efficient and responsible administration with dedication in spite of the huge pay and allowances they receive"[30].

It should also be noted that politicians and bureaucrats have different attitudes and perspectives on important socio-economic issues. Often politicians and bureaucrats make their respective positions explicit. Conflict any between them is resolved through mutual discussion. The political leadership would try to explain the rationale of a problem by emphasising the socio-political aspects while the bureaucracy would concentrate on the administrative and managerial aspects involved in it. The persuasiveness of the political leadership is a critical factor in amicably resolving the problem between them. As stated by a senior minister: "they may have difference of opinion, but they have no right to question. The best thing is for the minister to write down the decision in his/her own hand"[31].

Even in legislative committees the politicians and bureaucrats often express conflicting opinion. Many members of these committees have mentioned about this fact. The politicians have mentioned that they openly criticise the functioning of higher bureaucracy and sometimes such cases were brought to the notice of the Chief Minister[32]. This clearly shows that in a democratic set up, the political leadership has the upper hand in policy matters, because they are the elected representatives of the people and would always seems to represent the interest of the people. In other words most of the politicians express the view that in any conflict with the bureaucrats on policy matters the political voice would prevail.

However, the political leadership has conceded that sometimes the bureaucrats try to impose their own ideas. It is being done in a clever manner. The political leadership's implicit permission would have obtained for it. This happens when the political executive is too weak to formulate policies.

It is a fact that there exists a wide gap between the goals and the actual policy achievements. This gulf is widening with each passing year. According to a political leader the major reasons for this incongruity between policy goals and implementation are "faulty planning, lack of research, insufficient co-ordination between different functionaries, inadequate knowledge about development process and the absence of the appropriate policies and strategies for development"[33].

It is interesting to note that the politicians and the bureaucrats have advanced their own reasons for the failure in implementation of certain programmes. While political leadership attributes the failure in implementation of development programme to bureaucracy's lack of commitment, the bureaucrats in turn accuse of political interference in implementation process.

The survey very clearly reveals that the political leadership maintain the continuity of bureaucracy as an elitistic service and take pride in it. Further, the political leadership argue that the bureaucracy and its attitude towards the people has not undergone any significant change even after 55 years of Indian independence.

Another reason for the failure of development schemes is bureaucracy's lack of commitment arising out of the fact that the credit for the successful implementation would ultimately accrue to the political leadership[34]. The bureaucrats on the other hand strongly believe that political interference in administration would adversely affect the morale of the civil service, which in turn would affect the entire development process. A prominent political leader in the personal interview corroborates this.

With regard to bureaucracy's attitude towards political parties, political leadership maintains that generally they have contempt towards political parties. But at the same time they show their sympathy and affinity towards certain political parties. K.R. Gouriamma, Minister and prominent political leader agrees with this view when she states “they also have their own politics and in many cases find themselves loyal to some party in power. But in higher levels of bureaucracy rarely does it which affect the implementation of developmental measures”[=].

In coalition politics, which has now become a reality in the Indian politics, the relation between bureaucracy and political leadership needs redefinition. Coalition governments have been a distinctive feature of Kerala political culture for a long time. Since 1980, two distinct political formulations like UDF led by the Indian National Congress and LDF lead by CPI (M) have been coming to power alternatively. This has posed a major challenge to bureaucracy in the state to adjust with changing political situations. The survey clearly shows that after every government comes to power, bureaucrats in the top position including district collectors are being shifted. Even minor coalition partners have their own demands with regard to appointment/transfer of bureaucrats.

The survey data shows that the majority of the political leadership is of the opinion that the attitude of bureaucracy changes with the changing political leadership. For instance one CPI (M) leader said "when I was the opposition councillor in the District Council, the District Collector showed a non-cooperative attitude by not sanctioning certain essential grants for developmental activities[35]. A prominent congress leader also expressed similar view.

Democratic decentralisation and People's planning are some of the major developmental programmes widely debated in Kerala. Political parties, bureaucrats and other influential public figures have been compelled to make their stand clear on the issue. The Kerala experiment in decentralisation has been debated and appreciated not only in India but also outside the country. There is general agreement about potentialities of decentralisation in Kerala's development strategy. The difference between the politicians and bureaucrats about the programme lies in the methodology of implementation of the programme. This is confirmed by empirical data.

However, the survey also shows that, the majority of the political leaders expressed their doubts about the bureaucracy's commitment. The empirical data shows that the bureaucrats while supporting the concept of decentralisation expressed their apprehension that it might make inroads into their authority and more and more political interference in administration.

Kerala model of social development is in crisis today. The main reason for this crisis is the growing backwardness in the production sector and unemployment, despite its achievements in social sectors like health, education, literacy, public distribution system and communication. Whatever may be the reason for continued economic backwardness of Kerala, the politicians and bureaucrats cannot absolve themselves from this. A senior political leader observes, "Politicians and IAS officers are equally responsible for the lack of development and deterioration of the state economy. Most of the public sector undertakings go on loss because IAS officers man them without a vision"[36]

In short, the relationship between the political leadership and bureaucracy has not changed a bit. A proper relationship between them has not evolved over the years. The main reason for this is that both politicians and bureaucrats continued to hold their own respective positions without any qualitative change. A qualitative change in the relationship between them could be achieved only through an enlightened, committed and strong political leadership. Only then, the bureaucracy would change their attitude towards politics and development.

References

1. Narayan Hazary, "Political Executive- Permanent Executive Interface- The Case of a Developing Society" in R.D. Sharma (ed.) *Administrative Systems of Developing Societies,* New Delhi: Mittal Publications, 2000, pp. 143-144.
2. Herbert Morrison, *Government and Parliament*, London: Oxford University Press, 1964, p. 327.

3. Administrative Reforms Commission, *Report on the Machinery of the Government of India and Its Procedure of Work,* New Delhi: Government of India, 1968, p. 30.
4. Archana Sawshilya, "Politicians and Bureaucrats", *Prashashnika,* Vol., XXVI, No.2, July-December 1999, p. 77.
5. *Ibid.*
6. Ranvir Sharma, "Controlling Bureaucracies- The Present Day Dilemma in the Present Day Governance" in R.D. Sharma (ed.) *op. cit.,* p. 115
.7. R.B. Jain, *op. cit.,*p.182.
8. *Kerala Kaumudi*, January 11, 2002.
   - Interview data
   - Interview data
9. V. Ramachandran IAS, *Bureaucracy, op. cit.,*pp. 19-20.
10. K.F. Rustumji, "Ministers and Public Servants Make Uneasy Bedfellows", *Telegraph,* June 25, 1988.
11. N.C. Saxena, *op. cit.,*p.18.
12. S.K. Ghosh, *Indian Democracy Derailed Politics and Politicians*, New Delhi: APH Publishing Corporation, 1997, p. 361. For more details see T.N. Dhar, "Indian Administrative Service in Uttar Pradesh", *op. cit.,*p.38.
13. "Major Reshuffle of IAS Officers", *Indian Express,* October 5, 1996: *Mathrubhumi,* June 7, 2001; *Malayala Manorama*, June 21, 2001.
14. The appointment of former Chief Secretaries like S. Padmakumar as KSIDC Chairman; V Ramachandran as Planning Board Vice Chairman; C.P. Nair as Devaswom Board Commissioner and the recent appointment of V. Krishnamurthy as KSIDC Chairman after retirement are some of the examples.
15. Cited by N.C. Saxena, *op. cit.,* p. 11.
16. N.S. Jagannathan, *Bureaucracy, op. cit.,* p. 21.
17. P.S. Appu, *Bureaucracy, op. cit.,* p. 23.
18. C.P. Bhambhri, *The Indian State- Fifty Years, op. cit.,* pp. 168-169.
19. *Mathrubhumi*, March 3, 2001.
20. "Chief Secretary Retire on Suspension", *The New Indian Express*, April 27, 1999; *Malayala Manorama,* January 3, 2001.
21. For more details, see K.J. Alphons, *Making a Difference, op.cit.,* pp.88-99.
22. N.S. Jagannathan, *Bureaucracy,op. cit.,* p.14.
23. *The New Indian Express*, February 12, 2002.
24. C. Subramaniam, *Bureaucracy, op. cit.,* pp. 16-17.

25. *India Today*, September 26, 2001; *Kerala Kaumudi*, May 5, 2000: *The Week*, July 7, 1996.
26. Sukumar N. Oommen, " I Am Not Afraid of Speaking the Truth", *The New Indian Express*, February 15, 2001, p.1. also see October1, 2000.
27. *Kerala Kaumudi*, September 20, 2002, also see March 4, 2002.
28. Interview with Oommen Chandy MLA, Indian National Congress Leader, UDF Convenor & Former Minister, January 10, 2001.
29. Interview with K.R. Gouriamma, Minister for Agriculture, April 4, 2002.
30. *Kerala Kaumudi*, January 11, 2002.
31. Interview with K.R. Gouriamma, Minister for Agriculture, Kerala, April 4, 2002.
32. Interview with K.C.Venugopal MLA, February 2, 2002.
33. Interview with K.N. Jayaraj, Indian National Congress Leader, December 23, 2001.
34. Interview with K.P. Kunjikkannan, Ex MLA, Indian National Congress Leader and KPCC General Secretary, February 5, 2002.
    * Interview data
35. Interview with Smt. Jyothi. S, Municipal Chairperson, Payyannur, January 2, 2002.
36. Veliam Bhargavan, CPI leader and State Secretary. Details see *Kerala Kaumudi*, February 13, 2002.

6

Bureaucracy and Citizen

The relation between the bureaucracy and citizen is of considerable importance in a democratic society. It is the responsibility of the state and administration to create a balanced socio-economic and political environment so that the citizen could lead a meaningful life. Therefore, the attitude of the administration towards people should be democratic and on the basis of the sovereignty of people as enshrined in the Indian constitution. The government servants should treat the people with respect and show empathy towards them. This is possible only when the bureaucracy redefine its attitudes towards people by completely breaking the colonial legacies. The bureaucracy is supposed to sub serve the bureaucratic behaviour, however, towards people is being ordered on the basis of rules and regulations and hence acquires a dispassionate character. In the present chapter an attempt has been made to study the development role of bureaucracy and its attitude towards people as well as people's attitude towards bureaucracy. The data about the development role of bureaucracy have been collected from a micro level study of a sample of IRDP beneficiaries of Thiruvananthapuram district.

Before independence, civil servants seldom meet the public in any sense face to face[1]. Administration in those days was confined to the collection of land revenue and maintenance of law and order. In the post-independence period, governments have come quite closer to the daily life of citizens. The need and the opportunity for contact between them have greatly increased due to the welfarism and development schemes undertaken through Five Year Plans. A number of rural development activities increased because vast majority of people live in the villages. Any meaningful development in the country has to be channeled through village upwards. A nationwide Community Development Programme was initiated in the early 1950s with this aim. The National Extension Service was established with the intention of reaching out to the millions of farmers. A new strategy for agriculture development was introduced. Again during the middle of the Second Plan (1959-60) the idea of Panchayati Raj was revived, providing opportunities to the rural people to participate in self-government. Besides this, village cooperatives and commercial banks had extended services to the weaker sections of the rural community. An efficient public distribution system, health care, educational and family welfare programmes have enhanced the well being of people both in the rural and urban areas. A large number of public sector undertakings have brought the administration in direct contact with the citizens.

The extension of governmental responsibility over wide field of activities however fell short of its objectives. With the introduction of the new economic policy, which entails liberalization, privatization and globalization, the state and the administration, are redefining their role to suit the foreign capital. This has already sharpened the existing contradictions in the Indian society. Increasing inequality, illiteracy, unemployment, destruction of traditional industry and decline of agricultural production are some of the direct impacts of globalization. The government and bureaucracy have been so restructured as to suit the new environment. The bureaucracy's attitude and role should be understood in the context of privatization. The very objective with which we started parliamentary democracy, functioning on the line of welfare state with the help of political and permanent executive appears to be defeated. The governmental activities has thus broadened and almost touched all the aspect of individual and community life. This necessitated a change in the attitude of bureaucracy.

There exist a wide gap between the lofty objectives of the bureaucracy and the actual achievements. According to Ramesh Chandra, "there is a widespread feeling among Indian citizens that administration has not come up to the expectations of a welfare state and its performance in its dealings with citizens leaves much to be desired"[2]. It should also be noted that most of the developmental plans and programmes have not been effectively implemented. The discretionary powers, bureaucratic red-tapism, corruption, nexus between bureaucracy and dominant sections of the society including politician have created wide spread disillusion and discontentment among the people. The public is inclined to think that the attitude of the bureaucracy is not objective and impartial but explicitly partial. Thus the expected relationship between the bureaucracy and the citizen has been broken due to politicization of the bureaucracy. As a result, the bureaucracy has become dysfunctional and norms of neutrality and anonymity have become illusory. Complaints and favouritism to kith and kin of the bureaucracy as well as men of position and money have been openly talked about. The very expenses of the bureaucracy have increased. The citizen has inclined to think that the administrators are slow and there is a great deal of delay.

People continue to believe that bureaucracy has not changed since independence.[3] It is a common complaint of the people that the bureaucracy has contempt towards them. Any attempt to contact them with their genuine grievances has not materialized because of the arrogant and indifferent attitude of the higher officials. This behaviour of the bureaucracy had created anger and hatred among the people and has lead to their growing alienation from the system. As a result, the people do not feel inclined to go to secretariat or district administration with their grievances, instead they approach the politician for help who in turn act as a middle man or tout between the citizen and the administrators[4]. This is a growing tendency among the people because they believe that they can approach the politician freely and bureaucracy should take the blame for such developments. In this process, the bureaucracy loose touch with the people and their problems and remain surrounded by sycophants who tell them what they likes to hear and keep them involved in quotas, licenses and granting of small time favours. Several are the cases where these people exploit the poor public by posing that they are close to the collector and go on and make money in this manner[5]. Thus there exists a wide gap between them.

Citizen's Grievances with Administration: Corruption

People's grievance with administration has increased since independence. Besides delay, red tapism, indifferent and arrogant attitude of the administrators, corruption has become a major hindrance in the way of development and establishing a proper relationship between bureaucracy and the people.

Indian bureaucracy, like most other bureaucracy had its share of the corrupt[6].

However, there is a perception today that the proportion of corrupt administrators has significantly increased. Corruption is the misuse of public power for private gain or misuse of public office or disapproval of public opinion and the illegal use of public office for private gain. Corruption can assume many forms to cover a wide variety of transactions and operates at many levels[7].

Corruption operates at various levels in the public sphere and decisively influences political and administrative behaviour. It can do so independently among politicians and bureaucrats, but more commonly there is a nexus between corrupt politicians and bureaucrats. Politics and administration are inseparably linked. If the political environment gets corrupted, administrative environment is bound to get polluted. So there is a nexus between corrupt politicians and bureaucrats. In such a relationship both gain and each protects the other. The lower level operates as agents of higher levels passing up to shares in the bribes received at the operational level[8].

Bureaucratic and political corruption in India is a legacy of the colonial administration. During those days corruption at higher level was rare and corruption at lower level was prevalent among the staff of few departments like public works, forests, civil supplies etc[9]. During the Second World War due to scarcities of essential commodities, controls and rationings had been introduced. Numerous war related civil works and contracts were the main reasons for corruption in the concerned departments both at the centre and states. When these transactions increased in number and monetary terms involving crores of rupees, the corruption level also went upward bringing higher officials within its clutches. After independence both political and bureaucratic power started corrupting with greater vengeance and today cheating government is a regular phenomena and no more an immoral act.

Corruption was reported in Travancore during the princely rule. Several measures were taken to eradicate corruption under the *Diwanship* of Sir. C.P. Ramaswamy Iyer. Bribery was quite common in the police and excise departments and in the civil courts. In those days bribe giving as well as taking were punishable and this has affected legal measures to eradicate corruption. In August 1937, following the discussion between the Maharaja and the *Diwan*, it was decided that the Government would not proceed against persons who supplied accurate and authentic information on bribery and corruption. It was a practice with quite a few officers in Travancore service to receive supplies of provisions and vegetables without making payments. In August 1940, a circular was issued warning all officers against indulging in such corrupt practices and threatening those who infringed this rule with immediate punishment[10].

There is no area of activity, which is corruption free. This is because India is a low income developing country in which there is intense competition among both the affluent and the poor for scarce resources. Governmental involvement in socio economic development after independence has also accelerated the pace of corruption. The economic activities provided vast new opportunities for corruption to the offices of the government and various public sector undertakings[11].

There was every opportunity for corruption to get firm roots in the society. The low salary structure, the too many laws to regulate the day to day life of the individuals and impose of all kinds of social, economic and administrative restrictions on the one hand, tempting opportunities of illegal money making on the other hand and the lack of adequate vigilance, policing and support of political bosses who wished shares increased corruption[12]. In due course some kind of unhealthy nexus got established between corrupt officials and their political counterparts. Corrupt ministers generally dislike honest officers. They prefer to have more pliable officers as their advisors.

Unlike other states, the literacy rate in Kerala is very high. But industrialization and economic growth are lagging. The revolution of rising expectations unleashed in Kerala society, however, could not be matched with states ability to find avenues of employment, be it in the public or private sector. When opportunities are very few and demands are too many naturally there stand a chance for corruption and nepotism. Public officials who are in charge of regulations of such services will continue to face temptation and the officials may try to avail some benefits whatever opportunities their position provides them. The increased unemployment, demand for white-collar job, insufficient salary and ever increasing power being given to the bureaucrats to regulate economic and social affairs accelerates this tendency. The increased regulatory authority creates various opportunities for making money such as granting permits and contracts for construction works, granting import-export licenses, collection of customs and excise duties, sales tax and selection of beneficiaries in development administration. This type of regulatory functions increased corruption in various spheres of administration in Kerala.

India has acquired the notoriety of being one among the most corrupt countries of the world. India stands high in the list of most corrupt nations and at the bottom in the international assessment of human development. The Berlin based Transparency International ranked 99 countries on the basis of corruption in 1999 and India falls in the 73rd position[13].

An India Today poll held in 1997 reported that corruption was ranked as the greatest evil in the country above unemployment, rising prices, dowry, caste conflicts and even law and order. When asked, "how corrupt are Indian", 42 percent said very corrupt, 40 percent said some what and only 8 percent said not at all[14].

The Kerala Chapter of the Transparency International had conducted a survey in Kerala and found that among the various administrative departments, the Road Transport Department tops in corruption followed by Police and Excise. The least corrupted is the Animal Husbandry Department. The Public Works Department (PWD) and Town Planning Departments rank 4th and 5th. The Kerala State Road Transport Corporation (KSRTC) and Agriculture Departments are comparatively corruption free. For this study 205 respondents were randomly selected from 81 wards of Thiruvananthapuram district. They were asked to rank the corruption level in 25 departments. Most of the respondents wanted to eradicate corruption. Less than 7 percent of the respondents are of the opinion that it is not possible[15].

According to Vigilance and Anti-Corruption Bureau, Thiruvananthapuram, 22 cases were registered against IAS officers on charge of corruption. Against 20 all India personnel vigilance enquiry is finished. In the case of politicians, during the 1982-87 ministry, against 9 ministers vigilance cases were registered for corruption charges[16]. 202 vigilance cases were registered against government employees during 2000-2001 (See appendices IV-VIII) and 67 trapped cases were registered. Among these 102 cases were charged by Vigilance and Anti-Corruption Bureau. Among these 16 cases, references were send up for tribunal enquiry during the year 2000-2001. During this period against 436 officers departmental actions were recommended[17].

The Citizen Commission for National Issues, New Delhi, conducted a survey to study the day to day problem faced by people. The survey was conducted among the urban areas of the country. In a survey conducted in the government offices of the Thiruvananthapuram district in various departments like electricity, police, sale tax etc, the respondents said that they have to visit 3 to 4 times in the same office. The survey was conducted among 201 citizens who visited the offices for various purposes. Only 13.4 percent of them are satisfied with the service they received and 27.3 percent said that their work was done, 69.1 percent of the respondents said that considering the nature of the work the amount of time they spent is not justified. More than 45.5 percent of the respondents said that the officials they met are generally not so efficient, unhelpful and indifferent. 25 percent of them said that during their visit, officials himself or through subordinates or touts suggested unlawful gratification. Among the 201 respondents 27 percent said that their work was done and 47.7 percent said their work has some progress and 24.8 percent said that their work is not get done even after frequent visits[18]. Besides, the common man said that they have to chase from office to office and from seat to seat to get their work done. Considering the lower level bureaucracy, corruption mostly takes in the form of demanding bribes for providing legitimate services. The lower level corruption directly affects the people in general. The poor were worst affected by the adverse effect of this type of corruption and indifference of bureaucracy. They cannot pay or afford bribes in order to get benefits, which they are legitimately entitled.

The ultimate responsibility to check administrative corruption of the subordinates should however lie with the higher officials like secretary to governments and heads of departments[19]. Thus the common man does not always look upon administration with any good expectation of service to him. The citizen perceives that the administration is characterized by corruption, red-tapes and delay in the concerned departments and arrogant attitude of lower level functionaries. Since many of them are poor and unable to pay bribe as a consequence there is much delay in redressing their grievances. The common man is denied the basic justice in the hands of corrupt officials. This aggravate inequality in an already unequal society. Due to corruption and mal-administration the common man does not look upon administration with any good expectations of services to him, instead they consider it as a burden or a liability[20]. In a poor country like India what the people want from the political leaders is his ability to help them to gain a living and to stand up with dignity. What they want from the executive is protection from petty corruption and tyranny.[21]

District administration is the basic unit of Indian administration. It is basic because the district administration is the place where the implementation of developmental schemes take place and bringing the people, politician and bureaucrats into continuous interaction. The role of district collector has changed since the introduction of development schemes including community development and rural development programmes. District administration is the connecting link between the field and state level administration. In the processes of implementing various developmental schemes the district administration directly come into contact with the day to day live issues of the people. The collector is responsible for implementation of all developmental plan furnishing quarterly reports to state governments about the progress of the work. Collector also co-ordinates various other departments connected with developmental programmes. At the village level he also co-ordinates the various developmental schemes in co-operation with the local government institutions and people's representatives. The result is that district administration has a critical and crucial role in the development of the area. In short if the administration is to be meaningful it must be development oriented, it should address the concern and interest of all sections of the people.

In order to make administration development oriented, the people should be literate and conscious of their own problems. The district administration can play a role in the education of the citizens. The district collector can take up difficult programmes like literacy and provides the right leadership. The whole district follows him and success is ensured. The same concept is applicable to family welfare programmes. If the collector gives importance to the programmes then it will become a people movement and will be a success[22]. For this the administrator has to possess the qualities of initiative leadership and organizational capacities.

Similarly, in the implementation of development schemes in the district demands discretion and enthusiasm on the part of the officers. The higher official should exercise their discretion diligently, uniformly and to the interest of the people and not arbitrarily. Then only people can have faith and confidence in the administration. In this context it should be noted that the attitude of the lower level functionaries in the administrative hierarchy at the district level possess serious problems for establishing a proper rapport between the administration and the people. People often face a hostile attitude from the lower level functionaries. The people also express the feeling that the lower level functionaries lack any sensitivity to their problems and grievances. This situation often puts added pressure to the higher bureaucracy and this becomes all the more problematic in the context of politicization of the civil service.

A critical concern that would make the administration more development oriented is the transparency in administration. In the administration of developmental schemes there is nothing that should be kept secret. According to K.J. Alphons, a senior civil servant, "I do not understand why we have to be secretive in dealing with such papers. If a decision is taken based on objective analysis there is no reason to hide the decision from the public. The best way I felt was for them to read and understand what was being ordered. This way they would not be at the mercy of petty officers. This also ensures that the subordinate officials did not make money"[23].

Another difficulty, the people experience with district administration is lack of accessibility. As a consequence, the people's representatives and petty leaders in the urban areas have more access to the administration than common people. It should therefore, be noted that for effective administration it is imperative to solve the problems of rural people. It is with this objective various developmental schemes have been started by the government for rural development. The main objective of rural development scheme is to establish economic development. The World Bank paper 'Rural Development' pointed out that "it is a strategy design to improve the economic and social life of a specific group of people - the rural poor. It involves extending the benefits of

distinction of being major anti-poverty programme[27]. But on April 1st 1999 six self-employment programmes like IRDP, Development of Women and Children in Rural Areas (DWCRA), TRYSEM, Supply of Modern Tool Kits to Rural Artisans, Ganga Kalyan Yojana and Million Well Programme have been merged and a new scheme known as Swarna Jayanthi Gram Swarozgar Yojana was introduced[28].

For a proper understanding of the bureaucracy's role towards various developmental programmes and people's attitude towards the higher bureaucracy, a sample of IRDP beneficiaries had been selected and studied in detail.

Integrated Rural Development Programme (IRDP)

The IRDP was established on the basis of the recommendations of the Dantwala Committee in 1978-79[29]. The aim and objectives of the programme were identification of the families of the target group in each block, preparation of plans assisting their families, arranging credit support, monitoring the progamme of implementation of the schemes and follow up action to ensure that the beneficiaries derive long term benefits were by they cross the poverty line. The major objectives are to generate additional employment and raise the income level of identified target groups to make the families economically self sufficient and inculcate scientific temperament among people to achieve increased productivity[30].

For the effective implementation of the programmes, a heavy responsibility was placed on bureaucracy. It is a partnership of co-ordination between the bureaucracy and non-official agencies, which should generate the vitality for developmental efforts in rural areas. Chief Secretary was to monitor and supervises the programme. Further, this programme is implemented through DRDA at the district level under the chairmanship of collector[31]. The governing body at the district level provides guidelines and directives to DRDA. The identification of families, preparation of bankable plans for them and monitoring the implementation of the programme were the responsibilities of the block level machinery.

The IRDP strategy involves providing a package of activities to all working members of the families with particular attention given to economic progress of women. The progarmme covers mainly development of agriculture, animal husbandry, poultry, fisheries, irrigation, land development, village and cottage industries, self-employment schemes etc[32]. On an average six hundred poor families have to be provided assistance per year in each block. Out of them 50 percent families should belong to SC & ST. At least 200 beneficiaries in each block should belong to the industry and tertiary sector. Further, to ensure participation of women in the development process, it has been decided that at least 40 percent of the beneficiaries should be women and 30 percent of the beneficiaries should be physically handicapped. IRDP is a centrally sponsored programme funded on a 50:50 base by the Centre and the State[33].

IRDP in Kerala

The IRDP was introduced in Kerala as part of the national programme in 1978-1979 in 58 blocks. Later it was extended to all the 152 blocks in the State. According to the IRDP survey (conducted by the Rural Development Department in 1992), nearly 17.87 lakh families had been identified who live below the poverty line. As per the 1996 list, the families below the poverty line are 18.79 lakh[34].

During the eighth plan 2.42 lakh families were assisted. An amount of Rs. 206.54 crore was given as assistance. Investment per family worked out to be Rs.12535.00 during the plan period. The first two annual plans of the ninth plan witnessed a decline in the number of families assisted, compared to corresponding annual plans in the eighth plan, whereas total loan component and per family investment showed considerable increase. This is due to the shift from individual approach to group strategy adopted in the implementation of the programme. At the end of the eighth five year plan i.e. 1996-97 the primary sector assistance reached 41 percent followed by 34 percent in tertiary sector and 25 percent in the secondary sector. By the end of 1998-99, the share of the primary sector increased to 43 percent[35].

The framework of development administration in Kerala is basically structured with Rural Development Department taking the leadership and block administration providing the expertise in rural development. The rural development has a well-knit structure headed by a senior IAS officer known as Rural Development Commissioner. The DRDA takes up the development administration at the district level and it is responsible to Rural Development Commissioner. Below the 14 DRDA there were 152 blocks spread over the state. Co-ordination, supervision and training at the district level are performed by the DRDA while at the block level these functions were carried out by the BDO[36]. The task of the BDO therefore, is onerous. He has to operate at two levels viz. public relation as well as reporting to the senior officers.

Here an attempt is made to evaluate the impact of the programme in one of the districts of Kerala. Besides, the attitude of bureaucracy towards the people and people's attitude towards bureaucracy is studied through a structured questionnaire administered to IRDP beneficiaries. This enables to understand the implementation process of a major developmental activity.

For the purpose of this study, Thiruvananthapuram district is selected. Besides being the capital city where secretariat and other offices are situated, it contains rural and urban areas with SC & ST population. Among the 12 blocks of Thiruvananthapuram district, two blocks, one rural and one semi urban were identified. The semi urban block is Kazhakkoottam and the rural block is Vellanad. Kazhakkoottam is semi urban because a major part of this block falls into urban category while the coastal belt is rural in character. Vellanad is a hilly block and includes a considerable number of ST population. After detailed discussion with BDO and other staff, 200 actual beneficiaries had been identified from the IRDP list on the basis of simple random sampling with 100 beneficiaries from each block.

In the Kazhakkoottam block four Panchayat were selected, Sreekariam, Pangappara, Kadinamkulam and Andoorkonam. Among these, Sreekariam and Pangappara are semi-urban, Kadinamkulam and Andoorkonam are rural panchayats. In the Vellanad block, Vellanad and Vithura panchayats were taken for the study. Vithura panchayat has considerable number of ST population. The study area presents a true representative profile of the district especially with regard to various types of activities studied. In almost all areas the pattern of crop production was that of mixed cropping, mixed farming and multiple cropping. The areas have good transportation facilities covered by a network of motorable roads, rivers and rail. However, Vithura panchayat is comparatively backward in terms of transportation facilities.

The beneficiaries studied were categorized under eight heads on the basis of their level of education. About 57 percent have only primary education and 20.5 percent have studied up to SSLC. 16 percent of the respondents are illiterate. Only 5 percent had attended the total literacy programme of the government and they could just read and write their names (table VI.1)

Agriculture and manual labour are the two major occupations of the beneficiaries who possessed some land. Most of the beneficiaries had acquired their land through various schemes like Four-Cent Scheme, One Lakh Housing Scheme, Settlement Colonies etc. The beneficiaries of the IRDP schemes were identified on the basis of repaying capacity since, the amount distributed is repayable after deducting the subsidy contributed by the government. The assistance is distributed through nationalized banks. Majority of the target groups have the facilities like well, toilet, electricity etc. Some of the target groups have radio and television but newspaper is very rare. 33 percent of the beneficiaries came under the 36-45 age group, 29 percent are between 26-35 age group and 23 percent belongs to 46-55 age group. Average size of the family is four. Out of the 200 beneficiaries, 185 were Hindus, 8 Christians and 7 were Muslims. Out of 185 Hindus, 91 were SCs and 44 were STs, 114 females and 86 males.

For the successful implementation of the developmental programmes requires people's awareness about various schemes and full participation. The survey clearly shows that 78.5 percent of the beneficiaries are aware of development schemes of the government and 20.5 percent of them said that they are ignorant about such schemes (table VI.2).

Table VI .1. Educational level of the beneficiaries

Sl.No.	*Education*	*No. of beneficiaries responded*	*Percent*
1	Primary education	115	57.5
2.	S.S.L.C	41	20.5
3.	Pre-degree	2	1
4.	Graduation	-	-
5.	Technical education	-	-
6.	Post graduation	-	-
7.	Illiterate	32	16
8.	Literate	10	5
	Total	200	100

Source: Survey data.

In a related question asked to IAS officers, 72.2 percent of the officers responded that people are aware of the developmental programmes of the government. Only 17.7 percent officers believe that people are not aware of developmental schemes (table VI.3). According to one IAS officer "only literate sections of the society are aware of the programmes"=. According to another officer "An awareness of government programmes like IRDP/

NREP is perhaps not lacking. But the democratized laps involved in obtaining its benefits

Table VI.2. Awareness of beneficiaries about development programmes of the government

Sl.No.	*Awareness of the beneficiaries*	*No. of beneficiaries responded*	*Percent*
1	Aware	157	78.5
2	Not aware	41	20.5
3	No response	2	1
	Total	200	100

Source: Survey data.

parts off a great many genuine beneficiaries"=. With regard to the beneficiaries who were not aware of the scheme, the higher bureaucrats stated that administrators had tried to make them aware through education and public contacts.

Majority of the respondents opined that they came to know about IRDP schemes from block office, social workers and supporting staff etc. About 58 percent of the target group responded that they joined the scheme mainly due to their financial difficulty and failure to get a job. It is important to note that nearly 87 percent of the respondents made it clear that they did not get any benefit from earlier schemes. However, 13 percent mentioned that they had benefited from earlier schemes like housing, TRYSEM, total sanitation etc. At the same time they became the beneficiaries under the present scheme because their parents had enjoyed some benefits from early schemes.

Table VI. 3. Opinion of IAS Officers about Peoples' Awareness about the Development Programmes of the Government

Sl.No.	*Response of the IAS officers*	*No. of officers responded*	*Percent*
1	Aware	65	72.2
2	Not aware	16	17.7
3	To a certain extent	7	7.7
4	No response	2	2.2
	Total	90	100

Source: Survey data.

The political affiliation of the respondents was another area of enquiry. The survey data reveals that 67 percent of the target group did not have any political affiliation. Only 28 percent of the respondents stated that they had some political affiliation. It is thus clear that only a small percentage (17 percent) of the respondents stated their political affiliation and organizational membership (membership in Mahila Samajam, Balwadi, Anganwadi etc.) helped them in getting the benefits of the IRDP scheme.

Political interference in the identification of beneficiaries and distribution of benefits was stated to be low. Only 21 percent of the target group stated that there is political interference (table VI.4). The IAS officers associated with this programme stated that political interference is minimum. Only 25.5 percent officers stated that the political interference is a serious problem in the implementation of IRDP. Besides this, implementation of the schemes is constrained by inadequate finance, interference of the rural rich, ignorance of people etc. (table VI.5).

Table VI.4. Response of the Beneficiaries about Political Interference

Sl.No.	*Opinion of the beneficiaries*	*No. of beneficiaries responded*	*Percent*
1	There is interference	42	21
2	No interference	147	73.5
3	To a certain extent	1	0.5
4	Don't know	7	3.5
5	No response	3	1.5
	Total	200	100

Source: Survey data.

According to one senior officer "in the implementation of the IRDP there was social resistance from the middle and upper class and criticise it as a wasteful expenditure"[=]. Similarly another IAS officer responded that, " the real problem in the implementation of development programmes is the preparation of the list of beneficiaries. The officials entrusted with the job collude with the vested interests and include the names of non-eligible people in the list"[=]. It is also interesting to note that higher civil servants blamed the poor commitment of the lower bureaucracy as one of the major problems in the implementation of developmental schemes. The International Labour Organisation study team observed that one of the shortcomings is that targeting of the poor household is weak with the result that a substantial proportion of actual beneficiaries are left out[37].

The perusal of the financial assistance accrued by the beneficiaries is important to evaluate at what extent the intended goals were achieved. The IRDP finances a variety of schemes through a combination of loans and subsidies for households belong to the below poverty line. Under this scheme about 35 varieties of job were created for the beneficiaries. Among this, 64 beneficiaries started rearing milch cow, 23 beneficiaries started petty business, 18 received assistance for goat rearing, 11 beneficiaries started manual stone crushing, 8 beneficiaries got sewing machine and started tailoring units, 6 got assistance for banana cultivation, 6 beneficiaries for coir weaving, 6 for carpentry and furniture business, 5 for rearing buffalos, 4 for paddy processing, 5 for firewood, three received assistance to make country boats and two for starting weaving units. Some of the beneficiaries enjoyed assistance for more than one programme. One beneficiary refunded the amount as he got a government job before starting the work and one beneficiary immediately refunded the sanctioned amount.

Table VI. 5. Opinion of IAS Officers about Constraints in Implementing the Programme

Sl.No.	*Opinion of IAS officers*	*No. of officers responded*	*Percent*
1.	Lack of clear cut rules	11	12.2
2.	Interference from politicians	23	25.5
3.	Interference from rural / urban rich	5	5.5
4.	Ignorance of people	11	12.2
5.	Lack of adequate finance	16	17.7
6.	Other reasons	8	8.8
7.	No response	12	13.3
8.	Not applicable	3	3.3
9.	Nil	1	1.1
	Total	90	100

Source: Survey data.

Table VI.6 shows that most of the schemes drawn up for the beneficiaries were not productive in character. This is mainly because of the additional expenses involved in starting of schemes, which the beneficiaries could not muster. The study shows that even the target group, which received milch cow, could not maintain it because of several additional expenditure involved. Even the amount provided to the beneficiary is not adequate to buy a high-yielding breed. As a result the beneficiaries were forced to raise additional money from other sources like moneylenders. Moreover, the income received from the milch cow is much less than the total inputs required to maintain the cow. Similarly, the absence of support for construction of cattle sheds, inadequate grazing grounds etc. are major constraints. This applies to various other animal

Table VI. 6. Achievements of the Beneficiaries Through IRDP

Sl. No.	*Achievements of the beneficiaries*	*No. of beneficiaries responded*	*Percent*
1	Construction of house	19	9.5
2	Education of children	70	35
3	Savings	3	1.5
4	Chitty/Bank	11	5.5
5	Nil	95	47.5
6	Not applicable	1	0.5
7	No response	1	0.5
	Total	200	100

Source: Survey data.

husbandry programmes also. Similarly, programmes like banana cultivation, weaving units etc. were also have to face several difficulties. However, target groups started petty business and tailoring units were able to derive some benefits.

Regarding the role of higher officials, only 26 percent of the respondents agreed that they have played a major role (table VI.7). Five percent had responded that the collector is the most appropriate officer to oversee programmes for the upliftment of poor and weaker sections (table VI.8). A good number of the beneficiaries responded that the higher officials help only the rich and influential sections of the society.

Table VI. 7. Opinion of the Beneficiaries about the Role of Collector and other Higher Officials

Sl.No.	*Opinion of the beneficiaries*	*No. of beneficiaries responded*	*Percent*
1	Good role	52	26
2	Don't know	147	73.5
3	No response	1	0.5
	Total	200	100

Source: Survey data.

Table VI. 8. The Appropriate Officer for the Implementation of the Development Programmes According to the Beneficiaries

Sl.No.	*Opinion of the beneficiaries*	*No. of officers responded*	*Percent*
1.	Collector	10	5
2.	BDO	30	15
3.	Panchayat officials	8	4
4.	Panchayat member	13	6.5
5.	VEO	98	49
6.	Nobody	35	17.5
7.	No response	1	0.5
8.	Don't know	5	2.5
	Total	200	100

Source: Survey data.

The study also revealed that the higher officials have been completely alienated from the

Fig. VI.1. Response of IRDP beneficiaries about the increase in their annual income

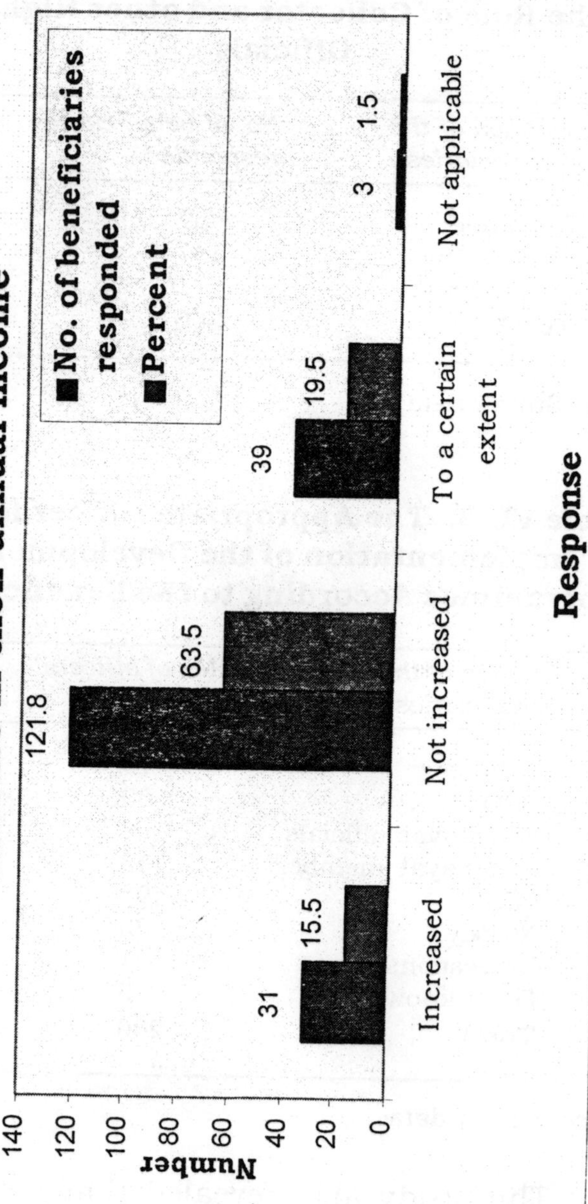

Source : Survey data.

Fig.VI.2. Response of IAS officers about the success of IRDP

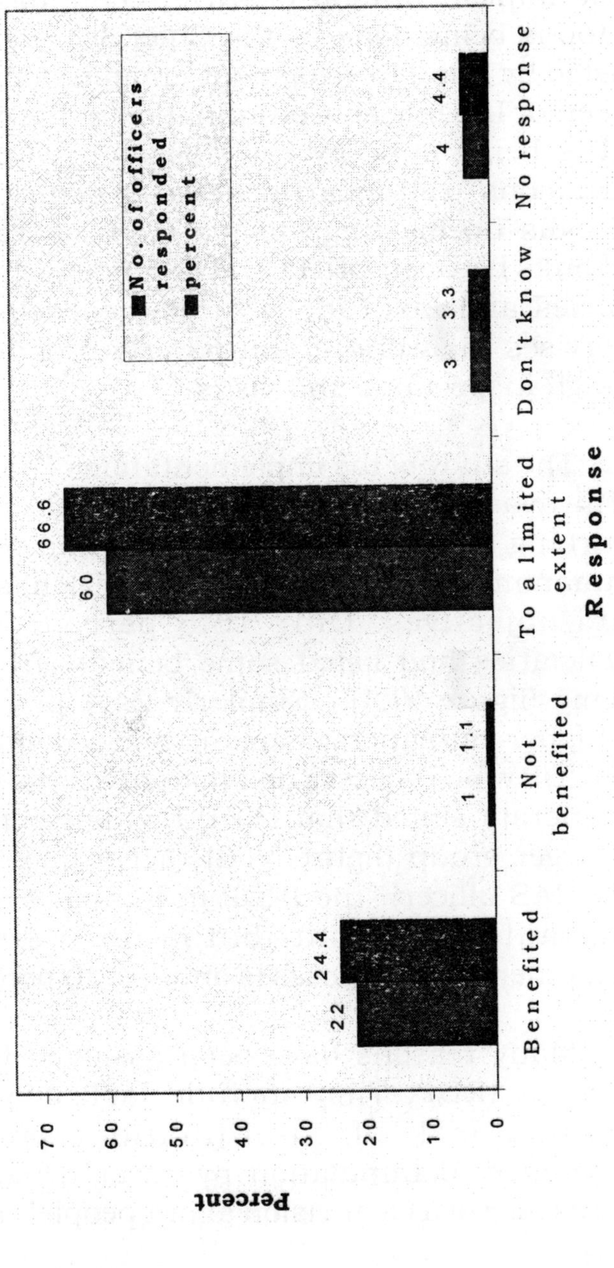

Source : Survey data.

people. With regard to the role of higher officials in the implementation of IRDP, coordination at the top is being done by the Chief Secretary and assisted by Rural Development Commissioner who is a senior IAS officer. Co-ordination at the district level is being done by the Collector, who gives instructions to all department heads of the district and calls up meetings to maintain operational level links between DRDA and other departmental agencies and institutions[38]. The collector also supervises the work of anti-poverty programmes through inspections and visits.

The study of the implementation of the IRDP in Thiruvananthapuram district reveals certain disturbing facts. Both beneficiaries and officials are unanimous about the fact that IRDP has failed in its objectives. Only 15.5 percent of the beneficiaries had listed some benefits from the scheme (figure VI.1). Similarly 24.4 percent of the higher bureaucracy has expressed the view that IRDP was a success and majority of the higher bureaucrats stated that IRDP has not benefited the target group (figure VI.2). According to one senior IAS officer, “the IRDP in Kerala is not an important factor contributing to the states development. The success is only 20-30 percent”[=].

Many reasons have been assigned for the failure of IRDP. They include lack of proper planning, lack of co-ordination, political interference, manipulation by rural/urban rich and absence of a clear vision about people’s needs.

Moreover, the total direction and control were in the hands of bureaucracy with limited participation from people. The guidelines issued by the government of India for implementation of IRDP emphasize active participation of the people in identification of beneficiaries and preparation of individual plans based on their skills and needs[39]. It also emphasizes that block level staff should consult with the family who are potential beneficiaries of the progarmme. Such consultation helps the implementing officials to determine the schemes, which would be most suitable in the area considering the skill of the beneficiaries and their knowledge of local conditions. Such types of consultations are against the inclined traits of the bureaucracy and bureaucracy resents doing it. Bureaucrats who implement these programmes have no previous experience of gauging the real needs of the people. The assistance provided to programmes which were not suited to the needs and experiences of the target groups lead to mystification of their assets.

The study of the implementation of the IRDP and the role of higher bureaucracy in it has clearly revealed the fact that bureaucracy's attitude towards the people and towards development has not changed even in a politically conscious state like Kerala.

References

1. Government of Kerala, *Administrative Reforms Commission Report*, *op. cit.*, p.132.

2. Ramesh Chandra, "Citizen- Administrator Relationships," *Management in Government*, Vol. VI. No.1, April- June, 1979, p.1.
3. Retna Bhattacharya, *op. cit.*, p.116.
4. T.M. Rao, "The Civil Servants are Not on the Job", *The Statesman*, Calcutta: November 9, 1980.
5. Alok Ranjan IAS, *The Collector Today- The Challenges of District Administration*, New Delhi: Wheeler Publishing House, 1994, p. 133.
6. Shekhar Singh, "Ethics in Administration" in T.N. Chaturvedi (ed.), *Fifty Years of Indian Administration, op. cit.*, p.71.
7. S. Guhan and Samuel Paul, "Corruption in India" in S. Subramaniam (ed.), *India's Development Experience*, New Delhi: Oxford University Press, 2001, p. 246.
8. *Ibid*, p.247.
9. Satish Tiwari, *Indian Bureaucracy Through the Ages*, Delhi: Rajat Publication, 1999, p. 204.
10. A. Sreedhara Menon, *Triumph and Tragedy in Travancore-Annals of Sir. C.Ps' Sixteen Years*, Kottayam: Current Books, 2001, p. 74.
11. Satish Tiwari, *op. cit.*, p. 207.
12. R.B. Jain, *op. cit.*, p.243.
13. *Ibid*, p. 238. Also see-Transparency International and Gottingen University Homepage, World Wide Web: http://www.gwdg.de/~uwvw/faqs97.html, p.1.
14. *India Today*, August 18, 1997, p.47.
15. *Kerala Kaumudi*, March 3, 2001.
16. Data from the Vigilance and Anti-Corruption Bureau, Thiruvananthapuram collected on February 2, 2002.
17. Government of Kerala, *Administration Report of the Vigilance and Anti-Corruption Bureau, 2000-2001*, Thiruvananthapuram: Government Press, 2001, pp.12-16.
18. Survey Conducted by Citizen Commission for National Issues,on March, 2002, New Delhi.
19. Satish Tiwari, *op. cit.*, p. 214.
20. M. Bhaskaran Nair, "Evolving New Values in Civil Service and Combating Corruption", *Kerala Journal of Social Science*, Vol: III & IV, No: 1 & 2 July/December, 1998-1999, p. 30.
21. K.F. Rustamji, "Ministers and Public Servants Make Uneasy Bedfellows", *Telegraph*, June 25, 1988.
22. K.J. Alphons, *op. cit.*, p.56.
23. *Ibid.*
24. A.R. Desai, "Rural Development and Human Rights in Independent India", *Economic and Political Weekly*, Vol. 25, No. 47, 1980, p.1975.

25. P.R. Dubhashi, "Restructuring and Reform of Indian Political, Administrative and Economic Systems" in T.N. Chaturvedi (ed.), *Fifty Years of Indian Administration*, *op. cit.*, p.106.
26. *Ibid.*
27. V. Ramachandran, "Development Administration- The Kerala Experience" in Padma Ramachandran and M.A. Oommen (eds.) *Some Issues in Development Administration,* New Delhi: Oxford IBH Publishing Co. Pvt. Ltd, 1987, p. 62.
28. *Economic Review* 2000, *op. cit.,* p.174.
29. D. Revinder, "Political Economy of Rural Development- A Study of IRDP", *ISDA Journal* 11, 2001, p.170.
30. M.A. Oommen, "IRDP Failure- Some Explanatory Hypothesis Based on the Experience of Kerala" in Padma Ramachandran and M.A. Oommen (eds.), *op. cit.,* p.102.
31. D. Revinder, *op. cit.,* p.171.
32. *Economic Review 1999,* State Planning Board, Thiruvananthapuram: Government of Kerala, 1999, p. 85.
33. *Ibid.*
34. *Economic* Review 2000, *op. cit.,* pp. 175-76.
35. *Ibid,* p.176.
36. C.N. Purushothaman Nair and M.K. Ramachandarn Nair, *Development Administration,* Thiruvananthapuram: Management Research Publication, 1993, p.146.

    = Interview data

    = Interview data
37. "ILO Studies Faults IRDP", *The Times of India*, May 30,1994, p.7.
38. I.C. Srivastava, *Challenges and Change in Administrative System*, Jaipur: Aalekh Publishers, 1999, p.182.= Interview data
39. S. Aravind, *Indian Administration*, Bombay: Himalaya Publishing House, 1992, p.186.

7

Conclusion

The role of higher bureaucracy in the socio-economic and political development of the state has assumed crucial importance in the context of the liberalization policies adopted by both the central and state governments. The study examines to what extend the higher bureaucracy who was characterized as elitistic and not development oriented has transformed itself as an instrument of development in the changed socio-political context of Kerala. The socio-political milieu in Kerala is unique in the sense that it is characterised by social transformation, higher levels of educational and health consciousness, radical politics and state as an instrument of socio-economic policies. As a result, the Kerala state with its very low per-capita income and agricultural and industrial backwardness could provide better quality of life to the people. This is what is popularly known as the 'Kerala model development' despite its limitations. It is also important to note that Kerala state has initiated the policy of democratic decentralization with a view to promote development with the active participation of the people.

Kerala is one of the few states in India where political parties with different and distinct political ideologies like CPM led and Congress led governments have formulated policies for bringing about socio-economic change on the basis of their own ideologies. The administration has also faced with the new challenges of liberalization of disinvestment and structural adjustment policy. The politico-bureaucratic structure of society plays an important role in managing public affairs by regulating production system and by intervening in the conflictual social process. All these development have necessitated a change in the attitude and perception of higher bureaucracy. So that the 'growth with social equality' could be realized. The higher bureaucracy which plays a predominant role in the formulation and implementation of development policies should be viewed as a powerful agent of social change. A study of the socio-economic background, their changing attitudes and perceptions towards development is of critical importance in this context.

The study reveals a very disturbing general trend in the socio-political and administrative culture of Kerala. The socio-economic milieu, coalition politics, ministerial instability, decline of political institutions and political parties and deterioration in the quality of political leadership has led to the bureaucratization and politicization of administration.

There exists a close relationship between the socio-economic background of higher bureaucracy and their attitude towards people, democracy, political leadership and the question of development. The study of socio-economic background of higher bureaucracy in Kerala establishes this linkage. The study reveals that 63.3 percent of the higher civil servants belongs to Kerala. Among this, three officers are Tamil speaking natives of Kerala. The remaining 36.6 percent hailed from states like Tamilnadu, UP, Bihar, Rajasthan, Andhra Pradesh, Orissa, West Bengal, Punjab, Sikkim and Delhi.

Another important point to mention is that 55.5 percent of the civil servants in the Kerala cadre belong to the urban background and 44.4 percent belong to the rural areas. In this context it should be noted that rural urban divide in Kerala is not so significant because of the continuous interaction between the rural urban population. In Kerala the rural, urban difference is comparatively less as compared to the other Indian states. Similarly, the study also reveals that the higher bureaucrats in Kerala belong to the recently urbanised and educated strata in the countryside.

The religious composition of these bureaucrats reveals that more than 71.1 percent of the higher bureaucrats belong to the Hindu community, 26.6 percent belong to Christians and

interference in administration are the result of a larger malice that had set in the post independent India due to the decline of political values and general deterioration of the society and Kerala according to them is not an exception.

Another interesting finding is that the coalition form of government, caste and communal pressures on the working of administration at various levels are on the increase and affected the efficient functioning of the administration. This opinion was expressed by the majority of the bureaucrats in the state. This is true in the context of coalition politics in Kerala where different major and minor political parties was masquerading in the guise of communal and caste interest meddling for their selfish and sectarian interests. This is clear from the study that only 22.2 percent of the respondents have favoured coalition politics in the state. Majority of them viewed coalition politics as dysfunctional to development.

About the character of the bureaucracy there is clash of opinion between civil servants and politicians. While majority (53.3 percent) of the higher bureaucrats believed that bureaucracy has transformed from colonial bureaucracy to development bureaucracy, the majority of the political leadership (65 percent) have rejected this view and held that the bureaucracy continues to be influenced by the colonial legacy despite the recommendations of various Administrative Reforms Commissions.

The relationship between the bureaucrats and politicians assumes crucial significance in a democratic set up. A study of this relationship would provide interesting insights into the working of the political and permanent executives. This becomes all the more important in the context of different roles that they perform that is the respective roles of policy formulation and implementation. Besides, the attitudinal and ideological perceptions of the political leadership and bureaucrats are divergent which might create areas of conflict and confrontation. The study shows that majority (70 percent) of the bureaucrats have stated that broadly there exists a good working relationship between bureaucracy and politicians. At the same time the bureaucrats are critical of the undue interference by the politicians. This clearly establishes the fact that while they are willing to work with the politicians for mutual benefits, they are aware of the political interference. In otherwords, the bureaucrats are willing to accept the political reality that exists in the state but at the same time their attitude towards politicians and especially the present crop of politicians has an element of contempt, which is characteristic of bureaucracy in general.

Political interference in administration is a major issue that vitiates the relationship between bureaucrats and politicians. Certainly in a democratic set up and particularly in a coalition system of government the role of political leadership and their interference in administration could not be completely prevented.

This is because they are the elected representatives of the people and their primary responsibility is to articulate the concerns and interest of the people. However, it is imperative to draw boundaries between the responsibilities and functions of bureaucracy and political leadership. Once the policies are decided upon, the permanent bureaucracy should be left free to implement these policies for the benefit of the people. Bureaucracy is also committed to the provisions of the constitution that is the welfare of the people. Therefore, an efficient and proper implementation of the policies of the government is the primary responsibility of the civil service. The frequent and meddlesome interference in the efficient implementation of various development schemes by the politicians would adversely affect the smooth working of administration. This would in turn affect the morale of the civil servants. This aspect has been empirically substantiated in the study. Nearly 80 percent of the bureaucrats contended that the political leadership tried to manipulate administrative decision to suit the interest of their political party, community and regions. The response of the majority of the bureaucrats is one of a meek concurrence to this kind of political interference. However, a few of the upright and honest bureaucrats express their displeasure to political interference by raising their objections by putting it in black and white in the files. But in most cases these written comments are ignored and superseded by the political leadership. As a consequence of this the officer who raise objection to the political interference in administration is invariably transferred to insignificant position. Officers who follow the dictates of political leadership are adequately rewarded by offering attractive positions. Besides, these planned officers are given re-appointment after retirement in public posts, liberalized postings in international agencies and multinational companies. It should also be noted that these officers always benefit from the ministerial changes between the two dominant political formations like UDF and LDF. This is done by posting their own planned officers in various key positions not only at the secretary level but also at the district level. It is clear from the above analysis that the politicians never encouraged the expression of free and frank opinion by the bureaucrats. The civil servants are denied the opportunity to express their opinion freely. This affected the efficiency of the administration because their experience and expert opinion were not given due importance.

In this connection it is important to mention the perception of the political leadership on the question of commitment of the bureaucracy. The study shows that the majority of the politicians believe that the bureaucrats are not committed to development and welfare of the people. They even stated that the bureaucrat's commitment to development is only 25 to 30 percent. This clearly shows that according to political leadership majority of the bureaucrats are still not development oriented.

Political and administrative corruptions are widespread in the state. This is the general impression among the people that nothing moves in the administration without bribes. There is a nexus between bureaucrats and politicians in corruption cases. A perusal of the various cases listed in the Vigilance and Anti-Corruption Bureau, Thiruvananthapuram, reveals that both the higher bureaucrats and politicians are involved in corruption cases. The studies conducted by the Kerala chapter of the Berlin based 'Transparency International' and the 'Citizens Commission for National Issues' New Delhi, to understand the magnitude of corruption and the citizen's grievances with administration established that the departments like Road Transport, Police, Excise, PWD, Town Planning are specially mentioned as the most corrupt departments. Besides, the study also conclusively proved the insensitive, indifferent and irresponsible attitude of the bureaucracy towards the people. The frequency of the visit and time spent by them in government offices are open and blatant display of corruption and a hostile attitude towards the people. As a result the common man does not look upon the administration with any good expectations.

Another important finding of the study is that both bureaucrats and politicians are increasingly found willing to formulate important policies and programmes especially liberalization, privatization and globalization at the behest of the aid giving agencies like ADB, IMF, World Bank, to create necessary environment for them to adopt such policies. Downsizing the bureaucracy, dis - investment of public sector undertaking, the curtailment of the benefits of employees and working class, and agricultural and other social security measures are indicative of external interference in the policies of the state.

A micro level study was conducted among the IRDP beneficiaries of Thiruvananthapuram district in order to find out the attitude of bureaucracy towards development and people as well as the attitude of the people towards administration. It should be noted that the real test of administrative efficiency lies in the effective implementation of the development programmes. It is also a fact that conflict of interest among bureaucracy, political actors and rural and urban rich manifest at the implementation stage. The study shows that 78.8 percent of the bureaucrats clearly stated that the implementation of the development schemes have seriously suffered because of the interplay of various interests. A major antipoverty programme like IRDP which, implemented properly would have benefited the poor and deprived sections of the society. Instead it failed to realize its objectives mainly because of lack of co-ordination between the implementing agencies, lack of proper planning, political interference, interference of the rich sections of the society and other vested interests. The study also reveals that the bureaucrats implementing the developmental schemes did not possess knowledge, experience and training about the needs and interests of the people. As a result the fruits of these developmental schemes have not percolated down to the actual beneficiaries. Rather the ineligible non-poor sections of the society cornered the benefits. In addition the developmental assistance distributed among the beneficiaries were not adequate enough for starting of an employment generating scheme. Result was that the beneficiaries were compelled to go to moneylenders for mustering the additional expenses, which in turn only increased their financial burden.

The study reveals an important perception of the people towards the bureaucracy. About 95 percent of the IRDP target group stated that the bureaucracy's attitudes towards common people have not changed. They continue to nurture an indifferent and arrogant attitude towards people. People also made an interesting observation that the bureaucracy is more inclined towards the rich and influential section of the society than the common people. The elitistic character of the bureaucray in all its manifestation is clearly revealed in the response of the people.

The pro-liberalization policies and in the context of state re-defining its role to suit the interest of foreign capital and their agents in Kerala would further sharpened the already existing contradiction in the society. Further, issues of development, social equity and welfare of the people would be the causality in this new agenda. Similarly the democratic decentralisation introduced by the government as an alternative paradigm of development is increasingly being undermined in the new context.

Suggestions

The study has raised a number of critical areas where the administrative organization and behaviour require radical changes. The most important question that has come in the study is how to make the higher bureaucracy functional to the growing developmental needs of the society and people. The development experiences of Kerala in spite of its unique features representing what is popularly known as Kerala model of development and high level of political consciousness has not been able to significantly change the structure, character and attitudes of the administration. This is mainly because of the lack of political will on the part major political forces and their governments. Even the left political parties which have enjoyed political power in the state despite the appointment of Administrative Reforms Commissions have not shown adequate political will to effect necessary changes in the administration and its personnel. It is significant to note that the first Communist Ministry headed by E.M. Sankaran Namboothiripad which initiated a number of measures to make administration people oriented could not complete its term mainly due to the pressure from the vested interest in the state who feared that the radical educational and agricultural policies of the government would adversely affect their interest. Subsequent governments, whatever may their political colour did not display their political will that was required to change the administrative system. The coalition experiments in Kerala by its very nature failed to create and sustain a development strategy, which would make the administration more responsive to the needs of the people. It is therefore imperative to change the attitude and perceptions of political parties and governments by creating a new administrative culture for good governance. What is therefore required is a change in the quality of political leadership as a basic requirement for a new administrative leadership and culture. The electoral reforms aimed at eradication of corruption in administration are an urgent necessity. Restructuring and reorganization of administrative departments incorporating new managerial technique and potentialities of information technology could be an effective way of making the administration transparent and sensitive to the needs of the society. The commitment of the bureaucracy to the ideals to the constitution and the people must be recreated in their minds through effective training and orientation. The strengthening of the civil society through democratic decentralisation and people's participation could act as a restraining force on the bureaucracy. Thus the people should play an important role through their conscious and effective intervention in the affairs of the state. This is possible only by democraticing the political system where the needs and aspiration of all sections of the society could find adequate reflections. Besides the right to information as a basic right of people should writ large at all levels of administrative hierarchy. This is the only way to compact the political and administrative corruption, delay and inefficiency. The nexus between bureaucracy, politicians, business class and criminals and undue delay should be eliminated. It is also imperative to create effective administrative machinery for the speedy redressal of citizen's grievances with administration. Decline of political institutions and values, which are the bane of democratic society today need to be corrected. The media instead of trivializing issues of development and highlighting non-issues should play a positive developmental role in the society.

Further Research

The study while making a detailed analysis of higher bureaucracy in development raises a few critical areas for further study. The present study has been completed when the process of administrative reorganization in the context of neo liberal agenda being implemented by the Kerala government has only set in motion. The nature and direction of these reforms and their impact on different sectors of the Kerala society can be evaluated and studied afterwards. Therefore, the impact of liberalization on Kerala economy, society and administration should be taken up for further study. The citizen's grievances with administration covering all the districts should be another subject for detailed investigation. Another important area for future research is the structure and role of bureaucracy appropriate to the new and evolving context of decentarlised polity and administration.

Appendix I

INDIAN ADMINISTRATIVE SERVICE
(Kerala Cadre)

Authorised Strength- Effective from 10-6-1999

[Government of India, Department of Personnel and Training (D.P. & T) Notification No.11031/1/98/AIS(II) A&B dated 10-6-1999 Published in the Government of India Extraordinary Gazette dated 10-6-1999.]

1.	Senior Posts Under the State Government	... 97
	Chief Secretary to Government	... 1
	Additional Chief Secretary	... 1
	Principal Secretary to Government	... 8
	Agricultural Production Commissioner	... 1
	Commissioners	... 5
	Resident Commissioner, New Delhi	... 1
	Secretary to Government	... 18
	Secretary to Chief Minister	... 1
	Director of Agriculture	... 1
	Secretary to Governor	... 1
	Director of Industries and Commerce	... 1
	Registrar of Co-operative Societies	... 1
	Special Secretary/Additional Secretary/ Joint Secretary/ Deputy Secretary to Government	... 15
	Joint / Deputy Commissioners	... 4
	Secretary, Land Use Board	... 1
	Director, Kerala Institute of Local Administration	... 1
	Inspector General of Registrations	... 1
	Director of Fisheries	... 1
	Director of Panchayats.	... 1
	Director of Municipalities	... 1
	Director of Public Relations	... 1
	Director of Tourism	... 1
	Director of Sports and Youth Affairs	... 1
	Director of Social Welfare	... 1
	Director, Scheduled Caste Development Department	... 1
	Labour Commissioner	... 1

	Director of Employment and Training	... 1
	Director of Civil Supplies	... 1
	District Collectors	... 14
	Additional Director of Industries and Commerce	1
	Director of Survey and Land Records	... 1
	Director, Scheduled Tribe Development Department	... 1
	District Planning Officer/ General Manager, District Industries Centre/ Project Officer, DRDA/ Cardamom Settlement Officer/ Sub Collectors Grade –I	... 7
		97
2.	General Deputation Reserve @ 40% of item 1 above	... 38
3.	State Deputation Reserve @ 25% of item (1) above	... 24
4.	Training Reserve @ 3.5% of item (1) above	... 3
5.	Post to be filled by promotion @ selection under rule 8 of the IAS (Recruitment) Rules, 1954 @ 33 1/3% of items 1+2+3+4 above	... 54
6.	Leave Reserve and Junior Posts Reserve @ 16.5% of item (1) above	... 16
7.	Posts to be filled up by Direct Recruitment (Items 1+2+3+4+6-5)	... 124
	Direct Recruitment Posts	... 124
	Promotion Posts	... 54
	Total Authorised Strength	... 178

Source: Indian Administrative Service Gradation List: 2001, General Administration (Special- A) Department, Government Secretariat, Thiruvananthapuram.

Appendix II

INDIAN ADMINISTRATIVE SERVICE, KERALA CADRE DETAILS OF SCALES OF PAY

(Effective from 1-1-1996)[1]

Sl. No.	*Particulars of Posts* *(2)*	*Pay* *(3)*
1.	*Posts Carrying Pay Above the Time Scale:*	
	Chief Secretary to Government	Rs. 26000 (Fixed)
	Additional Chief Secretary	do.
	Principal Secretary to Government	Rs. 22400-525-24500
	Agricultural Production Commissioner	do.
	Commissioners	Rs. 18400-500-22400
	Resident Commissioner, Kerala House, New Delhi	do.
	Secretary to Chief Minister	do.
	Director of Agriculture	do.
	Secretary to Government	do.
	Secretary to Governor	do.
	Director of Industries and Commerce	do.
	Registrar of Co-operative Societies	do.
2.	*Time Scales of Pay:*	
	Senior Scale	
	(a) Selection Grade	Rs. 15100-400-18300
	(b) Junior Administrative Grade	Rs. 12750-375-16500
	(c) Time Scale	Rs. 10650-325-15850
	Junior Scale	Rs. 8000-275-13500

Source: Indian Administrative.Service Gradation List: 2001, General Administration (Special- A) Department, Government Secretariat, Thiruvananthapuram.

Appendix III

INCREASE IN NUMBER OF HIGHER OFFICERS IN THE SECRETARIAT FROM 1969- 2000.

Name of department	Name of the post	No. of posts 1969	2000
Secretariat(Law, GAD, Finance, Legislature, Governor's office)	Chief Secreatary (IAS)	1	3
	Same Grade as Chief Secretary	-	5
	Additional Chief Secretary	1	5
	Principal Secretary	-	17
	Secretary	10	29
	Special Secretary	1	4
	Additional Secretary	4	78
	Joint Secretary	16	54
	Deputy Secretary	29	77
	Assistant Secretary/ Under Secretary	64	202
Police	DGP (IPS)	-	1
	Additional DGP (IPS)	-	3
	IG (IPS)	1	7
	DIG (IPS)	1	10
	Assistant IG (IPS)	-	2
	SP (IPS)	9	33
	SP (non IPS)	-	18
	Deputy SP	18	200
	CI	68	205
Forest	Principal Chief Forest Conservator (IFS)	-	1
	Chief Forest Conservator (IFS)	1	7
	Forest Conservator (IFS)	3	20
	Deputy Forest Conservator	7	35
	Assistant Forest Conservator	-	207
Public Works/ Irrigation	Chief Engineer	2	16
	Deputy Chief Engineer/ Superintending Engineer	12	46

Contd……

Name of department	Name of the post	No. of posts 1969	2000
	Administrative Officer	-	1
	Executive Engineer	64	174
	Assistant Executive Engineer	-	663
Land Revenue / Land Board	Commissioner (Member IAS)	1	1
	Commissioner – Manuel Preparation	-	1
	Additional Commissioner/ Secretary (IAS)	2	2
	District Collectors (IAS)	9	14
	Deputy Collectors	39	126
Agriculture Income Tax and Sales Tax	Commissioner (Member IAS)	1	1
	Additional Commissioner/ Secretary (IAS)	1	1
	Joint Commissioners	-	2
	Deputy Commissioners	4	30
	Inspecting Assistant Commissioner	11	126
Agriculture	Director	1	1
	Additional Director	1	6
	Deputy Director	6	111
	Joint Director	2	27
	Assistant Director	8	231
	District Agricultural Officer	13	-
	Administrative Officer	1	1
	Accounts Officer	-	19
Animal Husbandry	Director	1	1
	Additional Director	-	3
	Joint Director	1	24
	Deputy Director	2	53
	Assistant Director/ Sr. Veterinary Surgeon	1	383
	Principal Training Officer	-	1
	District Veterinary Officer	9	9

Source: Jose Prakash C.R., " Civil Service Yengane Valuthai (How the size of Civil Service Increased)", Thiruvananthapuram: Bharana Chakram, August 2001, pp, 12-13.

APPENDIX IV

DEPARTMENT-WISE BREAK-UP OF VIGILANCE CASES REGISTERED DURING 2000-2001

1.	Panchayat	..	24
2.	Revenue	..	17
3.	K.S.E.B.	..	14
4.	Health	..	12
5.	Irrigation	..	8
6.	Co-operation	..	7
7.	Fisheries	..	6
8.	Civil Supplies	..	6
9.	Education	..	6
10.	DRDA	..	6
11.	KSCSC	..	5
12.	Rural Development	..	5
13.	Forest	..	5
14.	Sales Tax	..	5
15.	SC/ST Development	..	4
16.	Kerala Water Authority	..	4
17.	Police	..	4
18.	Taxes Department	..	3
19.	Legislative Secretariat	..	3
20.	Hantex	..	3
21.	P.W.D.	..	3
22.	Devaswom Board	..	3
23.	Excise	..	3
24.	Municipal Administration	..	3
25.	Motor Vehicle Dept.	..	3
26.	Kerala State Cashew Development Corporation.	..	3
27.	Diary Development	..	2
28.	Judiciary	..	2
29.	Registration	..	2
30.	Kerala State Development Corporation for Converted Christians	..	2
31.	Coirfed	..	2

32.	Local Administration	..	2
33.	Handloom	..	2
34.	Archeology	..	1
35.	Higher Education	..	1
36.	Kerala Minerals & Metals	..	1
37.	Agriculture	..	1
38.	Nirmithi Kendra	..	1
39.	Animal Husbandry	..	1
40.	Kerala Land Development Bank	..	1
41.	Kerala State Co-operative Hospital Complex and Centre for Advanced Medical Studies, Pariyaram	..	1
42.	Pollution Control Board	..	1
43.	Employment & Training	..	1
44.	Malabar Cements	..	1
45.	Social Welfare	..	1
46.	Soil Conservation	..	1
47.	Wakf Board	..	1
48.	Co-operative Department	..	1
49.	Kerala Financial Corporation	..	1
50.	Indigenous Medicine	..	1
51.	Autocast	..	1
52.	Water Transport	..	1
53.	Legal Metrology	..	1
54.	Khadi & Village Industries	..	1
55.	Kerala State Co-operative Marketing Federation	..	1
56.	Private Individual	..	1
	Total		202

Source: Administration Report of the Vigilance and Anti-Corruption Bureau, 2000-2001, Vigilance (C) Department, Government of Kerala.

Appendix V

DEPARTMENT –WISE BREAK-UP OF TRAP CASES REGISTERED DURING THE YEAR 2000-2001

No.	Department		Cases
1.	Revenue	..	17
2.	K.S.E.B.	..	9
3.	Health	..	8
4.	Police	..	7
5.	Panchayats	..	5
6.	Corporations	..	3
7.	Forest	..	2
8.	Excise	..	2
9.	Indigenous Medicine	..	1
10.	Kerala Water Authority	..	1
11.	Civil Supplies	..	1
12.	Fisheries	..	1
13.	P.W.D.	..	1
14.	Irrigation	..	1
15.	Judiciary	..	1
16.	Pollution Control Board	..	1
17.	Registration	..	1
18.	Rural Development	..	1
19.	Sales Tax	..	1
20.	Animal Husbandry	..	1
21	Motor Transport	..	1
22.	Employment Exchange	..	1
	Total		67

Source: Administration Report of the Vigilance and Anti-Corruption Bureau, 2000-2001, Vigilance (C) Department, Government of Kerala.

Appendix VI

DEPARTMENT–WISE BREAK-UP OF CASES CHARGED

1.	Revenue	..	19
2.	Panchayat	..	15
3.	Kerala State Electricity Board	..	13
4.	Health	..	9
5.	Irrigation	..	8
6.	Agriculture	..	5
7.	Education	..	5
8.	Forest	..	4
9.	Industries	..	4
10.	Food and Civil Supplies	..	3
11.	Co-operation	..	3
12.	Rural Development	..	3
13.	Registration	..	2
14.	General Administration Department	..	1
15.	Employment	..	1
16.	Judiciary	..	1
17.	Home	..	1
18.	Kerala State Housing	..	1
19.	Police	..	1
20.	Public Works Department	..	1
21.	Sales Tax	..	1
22.	Scheduled Caste/Scheduled Tribe Development	..	1
23.	Fisheries	..	1
24.	Local Self Government	..	1
25.	Employment	..	1
26.	Treasury	..	1
27.	Kerala Water Authority	..	1
28.	Ground Water Development	..	1
	Total		108

Source: Administration Report of the Vigilance and Anti-Corruption Bureau, 2000-2001, Vigilance (C) Department, Government of Kerala.

Appendix VII

DEPARTMENT-WISE BREAK-UP OF REFERENCES SENT UP FOR TRIBUNAL ENQUIRY DURING THE YEAR 2000-2001

G.O.(Ms) 17/2001/
Vig. Dt. 28-3-2001
P.C. (P 2439)
S. Radhakrishnan

1.	Police	.. 1
2.	Health	.. 3
3.	Education	.. 1
4.	Civil Supplies	.. 2
5.	Revenue	.. 2
6.	Homoeopathy	.. 1
7.	Legislative Secretariat	.. 1
8.	Forest	.. 1
9.	Co-operation	.. 1
10.	AIT & ST	.. 1
11.	Motor Transport	.. 1
12.	Public Works Department	.. 1
	Total	16

Source: Administration Report of the Vigilance and Anti-Corruption Bureau, 2000-2001, Vigilance (C) Department. Government of Kerala.

Appendix VIII

DEPARTMENT-WISE BREAK-UP OF OFFICERS AGAINST WHOM DEPARTMENT ALACTION WAS RECOMMENDED DURING THE YEAR 2000-2001

1.	Panchayat	.. 68
2.	Revenue	.. 61
3.	Public Works Department	.. 47
4.	Transport	.. 29
5.	Kerala State Electricity Board	.. 25
6.	Corporation	25
7.	Kerala Water Authority	.. 22
8.	Irrigation	.. 20
9.	Health	.. 18
10.	Municipality	.. 12
11.	Education	.. 11
12.	Local Self Government	.. 9
13.	Police	.. 8
14.	Travancore Cements	.. 8
15.	Forests	.. 6
16.	Civil Supplies	.. 6
17.	Devaswom Board	.. 6
18.	Housing Board	.. 6
19.	Registration	.. 5
20.	Kerala State Development Corporation for Converted Christians	.. 4
21.	Sales Tax	.. 4
22.	Agriculture	.. 4
23.	Mining & Geology	.. 4
24.	CADA	.. 3
25.	Development Authority	.. 3
26.	Rural Development	.. 3
27.	Orientation Research Institute	.. 2
28.	Survey & Land Records	.. 2
29.	Harbour Engineering	.. 2
30.	Fisheries	.. 2
31.	Kerala State Financial Corporation	.. 2
32.	Kelpalm	.. 2

33.	Excise	..	2
34.	Law Department	..	1
35.	Employment and Training	..	1
36.	Tourism	..	1
37.	Labour	..	1
38.	Vigilance & Anti-Corruption Bureau	..	1
	Total		436

Source: Administration Report of the Vigilance and Anti-Corruption Bureau, 2000-2001, Vigilance (C) Department, Government of Kerala.

Reference

1. Government of India Notification No. 14021/2/97/AIS (ii)-A dated 17-10-1997 Department of Personnel and Training.

Appendix IX

The map showing the three administrative units, Travancore, Cochin and Malabar before the formation of Kerala

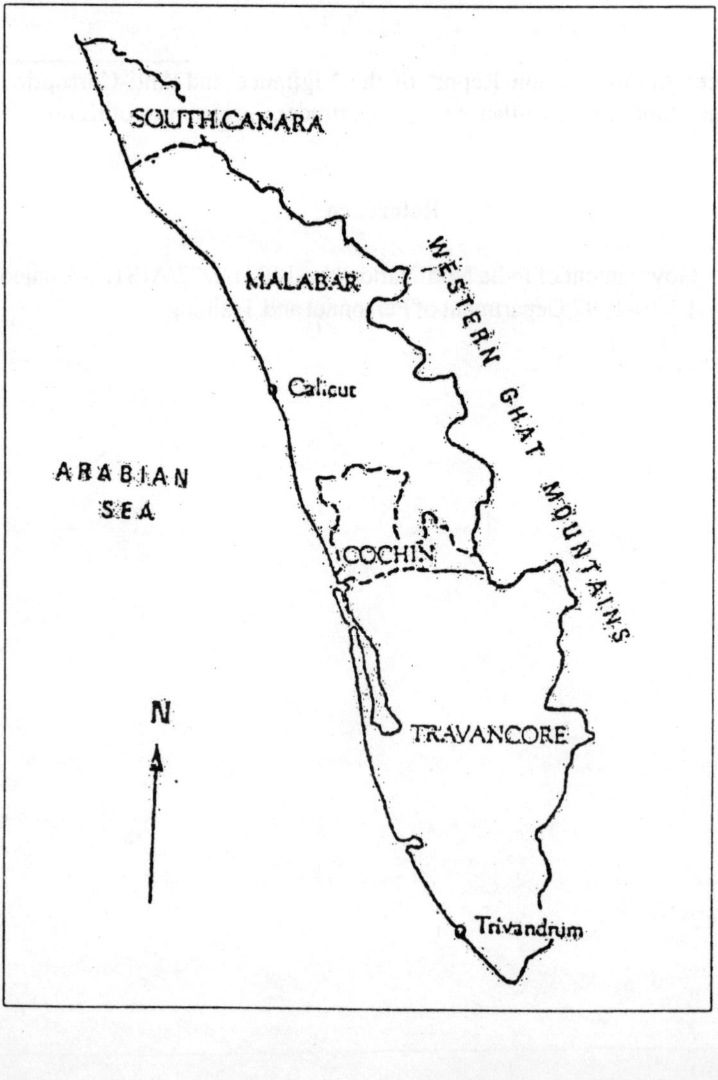

Appendix X

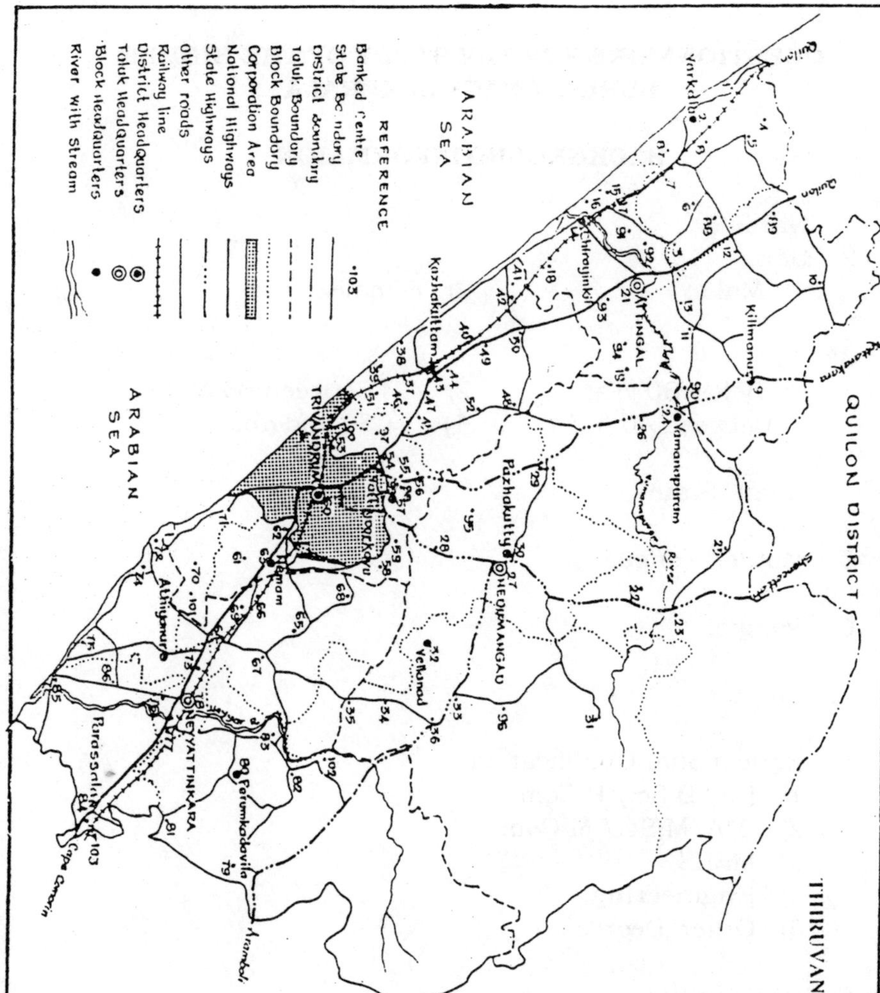
THIRUVANANTHAPURAM DISTRICT
QUILON DISTRICT
TIRUNELVELI DISTRICT [TAMIL NADU]
KANNIYAKUMARI DISTRICT [TAMIL NADU]
ARABIAN SEA
ARABIAN SEA
REFERENCE
Banked Centre
State Boundary
District Boundary
Taluk Boundary
Block Boundary
Corporation Area
National Highways
State Highways
other roads
Railway line
District HeadQuarters
Taluk HeadQuarters
Block HeadQuarters
River with Stream
Varkala
Attingal
Kilimanur
Vamanapuram
Chirayinkil
Kazhakuttam
Trivandrum
Pazhakutty
Nedumangad
Vellanad
Athiyanur
Neyyattinkara
Perumkadavila
Cape Comorin

Appendix XI

QUESTIONNAIRE FOR THE STUDY OF THE HIGHER BUREAUCRACY IN KERALA

BACKGROUND INFORMAION

1. Name :
2. Sex
   1) Male 2) Female ☐

3. Age
   1) Below 30 years 2) Between 30 & 40
   3) Between 40 & 50 4) 50 and above ☐

4. Home State :

5. Mother Tongue :

6. Religion :

7. Caste :

8. Educational Qualification :
   1) BA/ B.Sc./ B.Com
   2) MA/M.Sc./ M.Com
   3) MBBS
   4) Engineering
   5) Other Degree ☐

9. University :

10. Medium of Instruction
    In School 1) English 2) Vernacular ☐
    In College 1) English 2) Vernacular ☐

11. Occupational experience before joining IAS:

1) Teaching 2) Research
3) Executive 4) Fresh from College
5) Other Job □

12. Mention date of joining service :

13. Present position (Designation) :

14. Marital status;
1) Single 2) Married 3) Widowed
4) Separated 5) Divorced □

15. Spouse's occupation:
1) IAS 2) Doctor 3) Engineer
4) Teacher 5) Executive
6) House wife 7) Any other □

16. Occupation of the children if employed or you have in mind:
1) Civil Service 2) Doctor 3) Engineer
4) Executive 5) Any other □

17. Parents education:
1) Matriculation 2) Degree □ F
3) Post graduation 4) Professional degree □M
5) Any other

18. Occupation:
1) Teacher 2) Doctor 3) Engineer □F
4) Business 5) Executive 6) Any other □ M

19. Source of income of the family:
1) Service 2) House 3) Land
4) Vehicles 5) Business 6) Any other. □

20. If land is the source of income, how many acres of land do you own?

1) Less than 1 acre 2) 1 to 2 acres
3) 2 to 5 acres 4) More than 5 acres □

21. Did you participate in student politics?
1) Yes 2) No □

22. If 'yes' which student organization?
1) NSU I (KSU) 2) SFI
3) ABVP 4) Any other □

23. As a citizen and a voter , which political party or ideology do you feel closes to you ?
1) Congress I 2) Janata Dal
3) BJP 4) Left parties
5) Any other party 6) No response □

24. How did you decide your career?
1) Self 2) Parents 3) Friends
4) Spouse 5) Relatives □

25. Why did you opt for this career?
1) Career prospects 2) Social status
3) Service 4) Power
5) Salary □

26. What was your parents attitude towards your career?
1) Encouraging 2) Less encouraging
3)Neither encouraging nor discouraging □

27. What is your opinion about the training which the IAS officers receive, both institutional and practical?
1) Good 2) Very good
3) Average 4) Below average □

28. Do you think there is room for improvement?
1) Yes 2) No □

29. Do you think the medium of All India Examination should be in mother-tongue?
1) Yes 2) No □

30. Are you satisfied with the criteria of allotment of State or Union Territories to the Civil servants?
    1) Yes   2) No   □

31. What do you think of the system of tenure deputation to the center?
    1) Of use   2) Not of use
    3) No opinion   □

32. Do you think personal, ideological and political considerations influence the transfer of officials?
    1) Yes   2) May be
    3) No   4) Don't know   □

33. Do you find Kerala society and culture conducive to efficient working of the administration?
    1) Yes   2) No   □

34. Do you think the coalition politics in Kerala affected the smooth working of the administration?
    1) Yes   2) May be
    3) No   4) Don't know   □

35. Do you think bureaucracy has become development oriented?
    1) Yes   2) No   □

36. Do you think the character of colonial bureaucracy is still present in the administration?
    1) Yes   2) No
    3) May be   4) Don't know   □

37. Do you think the civil servants are the agents of social change?
    1) Yes   2) May be
    3) No   4) Cannot say   □

38. What is your role in the formulation of policies?
    1) Active   2) Moderate
    3) No role   □

39. Is it true that the civil servants offer advice or suggestions in policy matters to suit the interest of the politicians?
    1) Yes 2) No □

40. Are you independent in taking decisions?
    1) Yes 2) No □

41. What are the major problems that you face while implementing developmental programmes, like IRDP, NREP etc.
    1) Lack of clear-cut rules
    2) Interference from politicians
    3) Interference from rural/urban rich
    4) Ignorance of the people
    5) Lack of adequate finance □

42. How far the developmental programmes like IRDP, NREP, etc. really benefited to the people?
    1) Benefited 2) Not benefited
    3) To a certain extent 4) Don't know □

43. Do you think that people are aware of the developmental programmes of the government?
    1) Yes 2) No □

44. If 'no' what are the steps you take to make the people aware of the government programmes?
    1) Through education 2) Through public contact
    3) Through propaganda □

45. What is the attitude of the people to your new role as a development administrator?
    1) Positive 2) Not positive
    3) Indifferent 4) Don't know □

46. Do you think the development measures like IRDP, NREP etc. in the absence of radical socio-economic change would really bring about qualitative change in the life of the people?

1) Yes 2) No □

47. Who according to you should decide the development priorities?
    1) Politicians 2) Bureaucrats □

48. At what level the development priorities should be decided?
    1) National 2) State level
    3) District 4) Block level
    5) Village level □

49. While implementing the development programme, what are the problems you have confronted?
    1) Inadequate written rules
    2) Pressure from various quarters
    3) Opposition from the people
    4) Opposition from politicians and political parties
    5) Inadequate finance

50. How often do you have to exercise your right of interpreting rules?
    1) Often 2) Very often
    3) Rarely □

51. How do IAS officers get along with the officers of the State cadre in their capacities both as superiors and subordinates?
    1) Excellent 2) Good
    3) Fair 4) Poor
    5) Unsatisfactory □

52. What do you think are the reasons for conflict with other officials?
    1) Status 2) Seniority
    3) Party affiliations 4) Values □

53. What precisely is the nature of the relationship between the politicians and civil servants?
    1) Excellent 2) Good
    3) Not so good 4) Don't know □

54. It is said that generally there is a tendency among the officials not to displease the political leaders. Is it true?
    1) Yes 2) No
    3) Don't know □

55. What are the areas of conflict between the politicians and Civil Servants?
    1) Policy formulation 2) Strategic level
    3) Implementation level □

56. Do You have any confrontation with the politicians in your career?
    1) Yes 2) No □

57. Do you think the interference of politicians in administration hamper the efficiency of administration?
    1) Yes 2) No □

58. Do You find rural rich politicians and other influential sections interfere in the effective implementation of the policies?
    1) True 2) No □

59. How far is it true some political leaders look into administrative decisions for parochial ends, such as relations, locality, party factions etc.
    1) True 2) False □

60. At the district level how far administrative officials stand up to unfair intervention by political leaders?
    1) Often 2) Very often
    3) Rarely 4) Never □

61. It is often said that government policies are many times defeated due to the collaboration between the political leaders and administrators. How far is it true?

    1) True 2) False □

62. What is your level of interaction with the district, block and village political leaders?
    1) Often 2) Very often
    3) Rarely 4) Not so ☐

63. What is the desirable pattern of inter-relationship between bureaucrats and political leaders for better development works?
    1) Co-operative 2) Less co-operative
    3) Not co-operative ☐

64. The representatives of the people should have a superior position as compared to administrative officials in the decision making process, because they have a real understanding of people's aspirations and needs.
    1) Fully agree 2) Partially agree
    3) Partially disagree 4) Fully disagree ☐

65. The collusion between political leaders and administrative officials is harmful to development.How far do you agree?
    1) Fully agree 2) Partially agree
    3) Partially disagree 4) Fully disagree ☐

66. The concept of democratic decentralisation is praiseworthy but in practice, it is harnessed for purpose other than development. Do you agree?
    1) Fully agree 2) Partially agree
    3) Partially disagree 4) Fully disagree ☐

67. How far do you think Panchayati Raj has been able to achieve its goals?
    1) Fully agree 2) Partially agree
    3) Partially disagree 4) Fully disagree ☐

68. Do you think that political leaders should have a share in administrative decisions?
    1) Yes 2) No ☐

69. People often complain about the administrative inefficiency in government? How do you feel about this observation?
    1) Fully agree 2) Partially agree
    3) Partially disagree 4) Fully disagree □

70. If you had a choice, would you like to work in a
    1) District 2) Secretariat □

71. Do you think the public have confidence in you?
    1) Yes 2) May be
    3) No 4) Don't know □

72. What qualities are essential for a good official?
    1) Efficiency 2) Knowledge
    3) Commitment 4) All these □

73. Your commitment to
    1) Constitution 2) Government
    3) People 4) Self □

74. Is there any other thing which you would like to mention?

Thank you very much for your kind cooperation. The information furnished by you will be used only for academic purpose.

Jitha S.R.

Appendix XII

STUDY OF THE HIGHER BUREAUCRACY IN KERALA

Questionnaire for the study of relationship between Bureaucrats and Politicians (Answers may be given either in English or Malayalam)

Name :

Position holding

Ministers/ Former Ministers :

Member of Parliament :

Member of Legislative Assembly/ Mayor/ Municipal Chairman :

District Panchayat President :

Block Panchayat President :

Grama Panchayat President :

Members of any Panchayat Bodies :

Party Position :

Any other :

1. Who takes decision on developmental process?

   a. Politicians

   b. Bureaucrats

   c. Both

2. What is the role of higher bureaucrats for the formulation of policies?

3. Do you think that the attitude of higher bureaucracy has changed from colonial period to the present time?

4. How far the higher bureaucracy is committed to the implementation of developmental programmes?

5. What you think of the higher bureaucracy's attitude towards politicians?

6. Do you think bureaucracy is sincere to implement the programmes efficiently?

7. How far the political leadership takes the bureaucracy into confidence in the decision making process?

8. Have the bureaucrats ever questioned your decisions?

9. Have you experienced any conflict with higher bureaucracy in formulating and implementation of important decisions?

10. In case of conflicts, what steps you have taken to change their attitudes? Please give details.

11. Have you ever complained to higher political levels against the bureaucrat's action?

    If yes what was the response?

12. What are the various ways by which you influence higher bureaucracy?

13. Is it true that there is nexus between higher bureaucracy and politicians in the implementation of schemes?

14. Do you think that higher bureaucracy blindly accepts decisions of political leadership?

15. Do you think that bureaucracy is committed to policies and programmes of the ruling party?

16. Do you find that the bureaucracy can be loyal to any party in power?

17. What is your opinion about political instability in Kerala?

18. What is your opinion towards the bureaucrats response to "front politics" in Kerala?

19. Do you find that the bureaucracy is neutral in their attitude towards UDF and LDF?

20. Have you experienced any instance that bureaucracy is favouring a front?

If yes please explain

21. What is your understanding about the attitudes of higher bureaucracy when you raise the problems of people?

22. Is it true that the attitude of higher bureaucracy towards the people has not changed ? What is your opinion'.

23. Can you identify some of the actual reasons by which the bureaucracy does not show commitment in the implementation of the programmes?

24. Do you find that the bureaucracy is committed to decentralisation?

25. Do you find that the higher bureaucracy is happy with empowerment of grama panchayat?

26. Do you find that the bureaucracy is ready to work with panchayat leadership?

27. Do you find that the Panchayati Raj should have a separate civil service of their own?

    If yes give some important reasons.

28. What according to you is the ideal relationship between bureaucracy and politicians?

29. What is your opinion about the bureaucracy's attitudes towards people's planning?

30. Have you ever influenced the bureaucracy to change the decisions in a sectarian way, that is in favour of a particular community, caste or locality?

31. Do you think that the higher bureaucracy is corrupt? If so, give reasons.

32. Do you think that higher bureaucrats are efficient in their duties?

    If not, what steps should be taken to bring efficiency in top civil service?

33. Do you think that the morale of bureaucracy is badly affected by political interference?

34. Why Kerala is industrially and agriculturally backward?

35. What are the reasons for lack of development in Kerala?

36. What are your suggestions for administrative reform for efficiency and development?

Thank you very much for your cooperation,

Jitha S.R.

Appendix XIII

INTEGRATED RURAL DEVELOPMENT PROGRAMME – A STUDY

(A questionnaire distributed to the IRDP beneficiaries in Kazhakootam and Vellanad Block)

1. Name :

2. Address :

3. Panchayat/ Village :

4. Educational Qualification:
   1) Primary Education 2) S.S.L.C.
   3) Pre-degree 4) Degree
   5) Post graduation 6) Technical education

5. Age:
   1) 18-25 2) 26-35
   3) 36-45 4) 46-55
   5) 56 and above

6. Religion :

7. Caste :

8. How many members in your family :

9. Annual income of the family :

10. Any members with regular source of income:
    1) Yes 2) No
    3) If yes, how many members?

11. Whether you have own land?
    1) Yes 2) No
    3) If yes what is the area?

12. What type of house you own?
    1) Thatched 2) Tiled
    3) Concrete

13. Do you have any of the following facilities in your home?
    1) Well 2) Bathroom
    3) Toilet 4) Cattle shed
    5) Electricity 6) Radio
    7) Television 8) News paper?

14. Do you aware of the various developmental schemes promoted by the BlockDevelopment Office?
    1) Yes 2) No

15. Who gave you information about IRDP?
    1) Block development office staff
    2) Panchayat employees
    3) Political parties
    4) Social workers
    5) Other sources

16. What motivates you for joining IRDP?
    1) Financial constraints
    2) Inspiration from Block Development Office Staff
    3) Political influence
    4) Other reasons

17. Did you join in any other schemes before becoming a beneficiary of IRDP?
    1) Yes 2) No
    3) If yes in which scheme?

18. Are you a member of any political party/ organization?
    1) Yes 2) No

19. Whether the membership in political party / Organisation helped in getting the IRDP benefits?
    1) Yes 2) No

20. Do you feel that there is political interferences in the implementation of these scheme?
    1) Yes 2) No

21. Did you feel any difficulty from the block staff or bank employee in getting the IRDP benefits?
    1) Yes 2) No

22. What is the scheme started by you as per this programme?

23. Who gave directions to start this progarmme?
    1) Block staff 2) Friends
    3) Self interest 4) Village extension officer

24. Whether the scheme started by you was profitable and can be controlled by you?
    1) Yes 2) No
    3) If no what are the reasons?

25. Whether the amount sanctioned to you could be spent appropriately?
    1) Yes 2) No
    3) If not why?

26. What are the achievements made so far?
    1) Construction of house
    2) Children's education
    3) Savings
    4) Chitty/ Bank account

27. Whether your annual income has been increased after joining this scheme?
    1) Yes 2) No

28. Whether you have refund the amount promptly?
    1) Yes 2) No
    3) If no the reasons

    What are the consequences?

29. Who are the officers evaluated and suggested proper directions to the programme?
    1) Block staff 2) Bank employees
    3) None

30. Whether you have approached the higher officials like Collector, Sub-collector, Assistant Collector etc.
    1) Yes 2) No
    3) If yes whom?

31. At what extend these officers helped you?

32. What is your opinion about the role of these officers in development activities?

33. In your opinion who are the appropriate officers for the upliftment of poor and downtrodden?
    1) Collector
    2) Block Development Officer
    3) Panchayat President
    2) Panchayat Member
    5) Others
    6) None

34. In your opinion whether the developmental activities have any negative impact?
    1) No 2) Yes
    3) If yes whether the reasons are any of the following?
    1) Bureaucracy
    2) Interference of the ruling party
    3) Bureaucratic corruption
    4) Non-cooperation of the financial institutions
    5) Other reasons

35. Do you have any suggestions for the progress of this programme?

Gratefully Yours,

Jitha S.R.

Bibliography

PRIMARY SOURCES

GOVERNMENT PUBLICATIONS

Government of Kerala, *Indian Administrative Service (Kerala Cadre),Gradation List (As on 1-7-2001)* (Thiruvananthapuram: Government Press, 2001).

———-, *Indian Administrative Service (Kerala Cadre)Gradation List (As on 1-1-1994)*, (Thiruvananthapuram: Government Press, 1994).

———-, *Seniority List of Additional Secretaries, Joint Secretaries, Deputy Secretaries and Under Secretaries to Government in the Administrative Secretariat as on 1-1-2000*, (Thiruvananthapuram: Government Press, 2000).

———-, *Report of Administrative Reforms Committee (Interim Report: Part I)* (Chairman, E.K. Nayanar), (Thiruvananthapuram: Government Press, 2000).

———-, *Report of Administrative Reorganization and Economy Committee* (Chairman: M.K. Vellodi), (Thiruvananthapuram: Government Press, 1967).

———, *Report of Administrative Reforms Committee, Vols. I & II,* (Chairman- E.M.S. Namboothiripad), (Thiruvananthapuram: Government Press, 1958).

———, *Administration Report of The Vigilance and Anti-Corruption Bureau 2000-2001,* (Thiruvananthapuram: Government Press, 2001).

———, *Report on the Measures to be Taken for Democratic Decentralisation at the District and Lower Levels, Vols I & II* (Chairman: V. Ramachandran), (Thiruvananthapuram: Government Press, 1988).

———, *Committee on Decentralization of Powers (Sen Committee Report) Final Report Vol. I, Part A and B,* (Thiruvananthapuram Government Press, December 23, 1997).

———, *Economic Review*-1994, 1999, 2000, State Planning Board, (Thiruvananthapuram: Government Press).

———, *Proceedings of the Kerala Legislative Assembly,* Vol. XVl. No. 4, Vol. XXll. No. 29, (Thiruvananthapuram: Government Press).

———, *Bureaucracy,* Symposium conducted by Financial Express on October 6, 1986, (Thiruvananthapuram: Printed by Kerala Land Use Board, 1986).

Government of India, *Administrative Reforms Commission- Report on the Machinery of the Government of India and Its Procedure of Work,* (New Delhi: 1968).

Government of India, *The Gazette of India Extra Ordinary, Part I. No.290,* (New Delhi: Published by Authority, December, 2000).

Government of India, *Census of India 2001*, Kerala Part ll, The Manager Government of India Press, (New Delhi: 2001).

STATUES

Government of Kerala, *The Kerala Panchayati Raj Act, 1994*, (Thiruvananthapuram: Government Press, 1994).

———-, *The Kerala Municipality Act*, 1994 (Thiruvananthapuram: Government Press, 1994).

SECONDARY SOURCES

UNPUBLISHED Ph. D DISSERTATION

Bhaskaran, N.K., *Democratic Movementss in Travancore*, (Thiruvananthapuram: Department of Political Sceience, University of Kerala, 1983).

Books

Alphons, K.J., *Making a Difference* (New Delhi: Viking Publishers, 1996).

Aravind, S., *Indian Administration* (Bombay: Himalaya Publishing House, 1992).

Bansal, Premlatha., *Administrative Development in India* (New Delhi: Sterling Publishers, 1974).

Basu, Rumki., *Introduction to Public Administration* (New Delhi: Sterling Publishers, 1991).

Bendix, R, *Bureaucracy, International Encyclopedia of Social Science* (New York: MacMillan, 1959).

Bhambhri, C.P., *The Administrators in a Changing Society* (New Delhi: National Publishing House, 1972).

————, *Bureaucracy and Politics in India* (New Delhi: Vikas Publishing House, 1972).

————, *Public Administration in India* (New Delhi: Vikas Publishing House, 1973).

———-, *The Indian State-Fifty Years* (New Delhi: Shipra Publications, 1997).

Blaue, Peter., *Bureaucracy in Modern Society* (New York: Random House, 1965).

Bhattacharya, Retna., *Administrators in a Developing Society* (Bombay: Himalaya Publishing House, 1989).

Chaturvedi,T.N., (ed.) *Towards Good Governance* (New Delhi: Indian Institute of Public Administration, 1999).

Chaturvedi, T.N., (ed.) *Fifty Years of Indian Administration-Retrospects and Prospects* (New Delhi: Indian Institute of Public Administration, 1998)

Chatterjee, Partha, *State and Politics in India* (New Delhi: Oxford University Press, 1997).

Crozier, Michel, *The Bureaucratic Phenomenon* (Chicago: University of Chicago, 1964).

Denhardt, B. Robert & Barri, H. Hammond., *Public Administration in Action- Reading Profile and Cases* (California: Border Pacific, 1992).

Drez, Jene and Amartya, Sen., *India's Development* (New Delhi: Oxford University Press, 1999).

Dubhashi, P.R., *Administrative Reforms in Perspective* (New Delhi: Indian Institute of Public Administration, 1986).

Dwarakadas, R., *Role of Higher Civil Service in India* (Bombay: Popular Book Depot, 1958).

Dwivedi O.P, *Development Administration from Under Development to Sustainable Development* (London: MacMillan Press, 1994).

Eapen, Mridul., *Rural Industrialization in Kerala-It's Dynamism and Local Linkage* (New Delhi: Manmohar Publication , 2001).

Earnest, Dale, *Management Theory and Practice,* (Tokyo: Mac Grow Hill, 1973).

Franke, W. Richard and Barbara, H. Chasin., *Development Through Radical Reforms* (New Delhi: Promilla & Co. Publishers, 1992).

Ghosh, S.K., *Indian Democracy- Derailed Politics and Politicians* (New Delhi: APH Publishing Corporation, 1997).

Goswami, Sharda., *Bureaucracy and Administrative System* (Jaipur: Rawat Publication, 1998).

Jain, R.B., *Public Administration in India 21st Century- Challenges of Good Governance* (New Delhi : Deep & Deep Publications, 2002).

Jain, R.B and Heinz, Bongertz., (eds.), *Structural Adjustment, Public Policy and Bureaucracy in Developing Societies* (New Delhi: Har Anand Publications, 1994).

Jeffrey, Robin., *Politics Women And Well-Being-How Kerala Become a Model* (London: MacMillan, 2000).

Karlekar, Hiranmay., (ed.), *Independent India- The Fifty Years* (New Delhi: Indian Council for Cultural Relations, 1998).

Khanna, S.K., *Indian Administration-Problems and Attitudes* (New Delhi: Common Wealth Publishers, 1999).

Kunjanpillai, P. N. Elamkulam., *Studies in Kerala History* (Kottayam: National Book Stall, 1970).

Lasswell, J. Harold., *Policy Sciences, International Encyclopedia of Social Science* (New York: MacMillan, Vol.12 , 1968).

Lieten, Georges, Kristoffel, *The First Communist Ministry of Kerala 1957-58* (New Delhi: KP Bagh & Co., 1982).

Maheswari, S.R., *A History of Indian Administration* (New Delhi: Orient Long Man Limited, 2001).

———-, *Comparative Government and Politics* (Agra: Lekshmi Narayan Agarwal Educational Publications, 1983).

Menon, A. Sreedharan., *A Survey of Kerala History* (Madras: S. Viswanathan Printer & Publisher, 1994).

———-, *Kerala and Freedom Struggle* (Kottayam: DC Books, 1997).

————, *Triumph and Tragedy in Travancore-Annals of Sir CPs' Sixteen Years* (Kottayam: Current Books, 2001).

Menon, C. Achuthan., *Cochin State Manuel* (Ernakulam: 1941).

Michel, R., *Political Parties- A Sociological Study of Modern Democracy* (New York: Dover Publishers, 1959).

Misra, B.B., *The Bureaucracy in India – A Historical Analysis of Development Up to 1947* (New York: Oxford University Press, 1977).

Montgomery, John and William, Siffin.,(eds.) *Approaches to Development- Politics, Administration and Change* (New York: Mc Grow Hill, 1966).

Morison, Herbert., *Government and Parliament* (London: Oxford University Press, 1964).

Nair, A. Balakrishnan., *Landmark in the Administration of Kerala* (Thiruvananthapuram: Indian Institute of Public Administration Regional Branch, 1996).

Nair, C.N. Purushothaman and Ramachandran, Nair M.K., *Development Administration* (Thiruvananthapuram: Management Research Publication, 1993).

Nair, K. Sukumaran., *Administrative Co-ordination at State Level in India- A Study of Government Secretariat and Board of Revenue in Kerala* (Thiruvananthapuram: Kerala Academy of Political Science, 1975).

Nair, V. Balakrishnan., *Social Development and Demographic Changes in South India* (New Delhi: MP Publishing Pvt. LTD, 1994).

Namboothiripad, E.M.S., *Kerala Charithram Marxist Veekshanathil*, (M), (Thiruvanthapuram: Chintha Publication, 1997).

Nossitter, T.J., *Communism in Kerala- A Study of Political Adaptation* (New Delhi: Oxford University Press, 1982).

———-, *Marxist State Government in India- Politics, Economics and Society* (London: Pinter Publishers, 1988).

Oommen, M.A., *Rethinking Development- Kerala's Development Experiences* (New Delhi : Concept Publishing Company, 1999 Vol, 1 & 2).

Pai, Panandikar, V.A., *Policy Science and Policy Making in India* (New Delhi: Centre for Policy Research, 1988).

Pai, Panandikar, V.A and Kshir, Sagar, S.S., (eds.) *Bureaucracy and Development Administration* (New Delhi: Centre for Policy Research, 1978).

Pai, Panandikar, V.A., Bishnoi, R.N & Sharma, O.P.,(eds.) *Development Bureaucracy* (New Delhi: Oxford IBH Publishing Company, 1983).

Palombara, La, Joseph., (ed.) *Bureaucracy and Political Development* (New Jersey: Princeton University Press, 1963).

Parayil, Govindan., (ed) *Kerala- The Development Experience- Reflections on Sustainability and Replicability* (London ZED Books, 2000).

Prabhsh, J., *Affirmative Action & Social Change – Social Mobility of Dalits* (New Delhi: Anmol Publications Pvt. Ltd., 2001).

Prakash, B.A., *Kerala's Economic Development Issues and Problems* (New Delhi: Sage Publications, 1994).

Prasad, B., *Indian Administrative Service* (New Delhi: S. Chand & Co., 1968).

Radhakrishnan, P., *Peasent Struggle- Land Reforms and Social Changes in Malabar 1836-1982* (New Delhi: Sage Publication, 1989).

Ramachadran, Padma & Oommen, M.A., *Some Issues in Development Administration* (Oxford IBH Publishing Co. Ltd., 1987).

Rao, Ramakanth & Prasanth, K. Mathur., *Advanced Public Administration -Policy Planning and Decision Making,* Vol. 1 & 2 (New Delhi, Kanishka Publishers, 1994).

Sadasivan, S.N., *Administration and Social Development in Kerala* (Thiruvananthapuram: Indian Institute of Public Administration, Regional Branch, 1988).

———-, *Administrative Integration of Kerala* (Thiruvananthapuram: Indian Institute of Public Administration, Regional Branch, 1986).

Sapru, R.K., *Development Administration* (New Delhi: Deep & Deep Publications, 1994).

———-, *Civil Service Administration in India* (New Delhi: Deep & Deep Publications, 1985).

Saradamani, K., *Matriliny Transferred* (New Delhi: Sage publication, 1999).

Sharma, R.D., (ed.) *Administrative System of Developing Societies* (New Delhi: Mithal Publication , 2000).

Stone, C. Donald., (ed.) *Education for Development Administration* (Brussels: International Institute of Administrative Science, 1966).

Srivasthava, I.C., *Challenges and Changes in Administrative System* (Jaipur: Aalekh Publishers, 1999).

Subramaniam, S., (ed.) *India's Development Experiences* (New Delhi: Oxford University Press, 2001).

Subramaniam, V., (ed.) *Social, Background of India's Administrators* (New Delhi: Publication Division, Ministry of Information and Broadcasting Division Government of India, 1977).

Tandau, C. Alfred., *Policy Implementation in India* (New Delhi: Vikas Publishers, 1996).

Tiwari, Satheesh., *Indian Bureaucracy Through the Ages* (New Delhi: Rajath Publication, 1999).

Mathur, Kuldeep., "Top Civil Servant's Path to Success", *Economic Times*, April 28, 1987.

Nair, M. Bhaskaran., "Evolving New Values in Civil Service and Combating Corruption", *Kerala Journal of Social Science*, Vol. III & IV No. 1 & 2, 1998-1999.

Nayar, Kuldeep., " Politicised Bureaucracy", *Telegraph*, January 4, 1990.

Oommen, M.A., " Kerala and the New World Order", *Mainstream*, No-99, 1994.

Oommen, N Sukumar., "I Am Not Afraid of Speaking the Truth", *The New Indian Express*, February 15, 2001.

Raghavendra, Rao, Meera., "Professionalism in IAS", *The Hindu*, July 5, 1994.

Ramachandran, Padma., "Women in Politics and Governance", *VMFT Newsletter* (A Publication of Vakkom Moulavi Foundation Trust), Vol. 7 (1), 1995.

Ramachandran, Rajesh., "Wounded Yet Unrepenting - K.J Alphons Suspended From the IAS for Writing an Explosive Article", *The Week*, July 7, 1996.

Remesh, Chandra., "Citizen Administrator Relationship" *Management in Government*, Vol. VI. No.1, April –June 1979.

Rao, T.M., "The Civil Servants are Not on the Job", *The Statesmen*, November 9, 1980.

Revindar, D., "Political Economy of Rural Development- A Study of IRDP", *Institute for the Study of Developing Areas (ISDA) Journal II(4)October-December*, 2001.

Rustamji, K.M., " Ministers and Public Servants Make Uneasy Bedfellows" *Telegraph*, June 25, 1988.

Sadanandan, K., "Politicization of the Bureaucracy", *The Hindu,* March 24, 1992.

Sawshilya, Archana., " Politicians and Bureaucrats", *Prashashnika,* Vol. XXVI (2), July - December, 1999.

Saxena, N.C., "Administration and the People– Higher Bureaucracy- Need for Radical Reforms", *Management in Government,* Vol. 32, No.3 October-December, 2002.

Sinha, Letha., " Role and Rationale of All India Services", *Indian Journal of Public Administration,* Vol. XXVI, No. 4, October-December, 1990.

Sundaram, S.S. Meenakshi., "Public Service Reform", *Seminar,* No. 514, June 2002.

Sureshkumar, R.K., "Combating Administrative Inefficiency in Kerala: Revamping the Second Layer of Administration", *Institute for the Study of Developing Areas (ISDA) Journal,* Vol. 4 No.3 July-December, 1999.

Trivedi, R.K., & Rao, D.N., "Regular Recruits to IAS- A Study" ,*Journal of National Academy of Administration,* Vol. 3, 1960.

Victor, A. Thompson., "Administrative Objection for Development Administration", *Administrative Science Quarterly,* Vol.9 , July 1964.

RESEARCH JOURNALS

Administrator (Mussoori)
Administrative Science Quarterly (New Delhi)
Economic and Political Weekly (New Delhi)
Indian Journal of Political Science (New Delhi)
Indian Journal of Public Administration (New Delhi)

Index